Crime Scene Tour: San Francisco

I0135261

Eric Golembiewski

Crime Scene Tour: San Francisco

Copyright © 2020 Eric Golembiewski

All Rights Reserved. No part of this book may be reproduced in any form, or by any electronic, mechanical, or other means, without permission in writing from the publisher.

For information regarding permissions, contact Intryoli Press

I work to ensure this book has information as accurate as possible. Most of the stories have been covered by newspapers, and the legends have been reproduced many times. Many of the stories in this book are common to our culture. Life evolves and today's occupants may be different than those from the past. Finally, this book is a guide to crimes scenes and history. The author and publisher have no control over and assume no responsibility for anyone's safety.

978-0-9993151-6-3

First edition, first printing, 2020

Publisher's Cataloging-in-Publication Data

Golembiewski, Eric

Crime Scene Tour: San Francisco.

/ Eric Golembiewski. –1st ed.

p. cm.

1. Crime stories, True. 2. San Francisco Tourist Guides, manuals, etc. 3. San Francisco history.

364.1523

2020

Table of Contents

Introduction

❦

San Francisco is home to three quarters of a million residents living in a seven mile by seven mile metropolis on a peninsula jutting into the Pacific Ocean. Twenty five million people visit the city in a year to do business and see the sights like the Golden Gate Bridge, Chinatown, City Hall, and the Transamerica Pyramid.

For those who have had enough conventional tourism, this book offers a different path. *Crime Scene Tour: San Francisco* provides a fresh look at the city, and the true-crimes that shaped it. The 108 historical crime sights are organized into seven geographical tours.

Enjoy the tour through historical crime.

Conventional History

California and San Francisco's conventional history began long before the Europeans arrived. Native Americans hunted and fished on a sandy peninsula jutting into the Pacific. Europeans came from all directions. Russians came south from their Alaskan territory in search of furs. Spaniards came north from their Central and South American territories in search of gold and souls. The British came east from their travels of conquest in the Pacific. Americans came west in search of land and fortune.

San Francisco started in an excellent position to become a great metropolis. It was a protected port, which provided access to California's inland where people mined the riches of the land. The city grew up fast, and became its own society with its own business. Fast growth comes at a cost, and the city has always had a boom and bust way about it that never lets anyone forget the Goldrush. The social changes came with physical changes to the very land of San Francisco as grass and pavement covered the sand and scrub.

San Francisco's crime history happened along with its conventional history. Here are some key events in the city's history.

1542 Juan Rodriguez Cabrillo discovered the Farallones, a set of islands outside the Bay.

1579 Sir Francis Drake sailed into the Bay and claimed it for England.

1776 Juan Bautista de Anza of Spain built the site of the now Mission Delores in the Mission District   while the Spanish Military built what has become the Presidio. San Francisco of today began.

1821 Mexico breaks free from Spain and San Francisco becomes a part of Mexico.

1835 The Pueblo of Yerba Buena was founded.

1846 The Mexican American War began. Mexico lost parts of California including San Francisco.

1847 Residents renamed Yerba Buena as San Francisco.

1848 Gold was discovered at Sutter's Mill in Northern California.

1850 San Francisco was incorporated. California became the thirty first state in the Union.

1865 An earthquake hit, causing damage.

1868 An earthquake hit causing more damage than the previous.

1869 The Transcontinental Railroad was completed, connecting San Francisco Bay with the rail networks of the east.

1906 A magnitude 8.25 earthquake hit causing near total destruction.

1915 San Francisco hosted the Panama International Exposition in the Marina District.

1937 The Golden Gate Bridge opened.

1945 The United Nations Charters was created and signed in San Francisco.

1969 San Francisco had its Summer of Love.

1989 A 7.1 magnitude earthquake hit causing billions of dollars in damage to the area.

2008 The US entered the Great Recession, and San Francisco outperformed the nationwide average to recover based mostly on its tech industries.

Map

San Francisco
Crime Scene Tour
Map of Districts

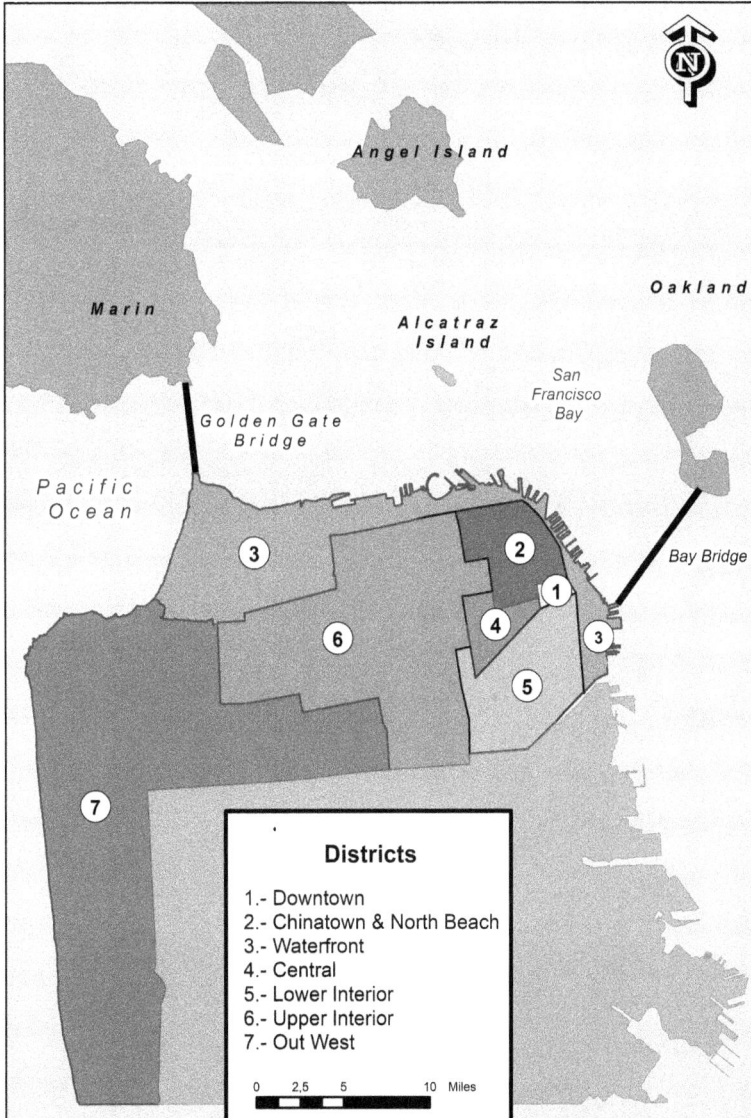

Angel Island

Marin

Oakland

Alcatraz Island

San Francisco Bay

Golden Gate Bridge

Pacific Ocean

③

②

①

④ ③

⑥

⑤

Bay Bridge

⑦

Districts

1.- Downtown
2.- Chinatown & North Beach
3.- Waterfront
4.- Central
5.- Lower Interior
6.- Upper Interior
7.- Out West

0   2,5   5   10   Miles

1. Downtown

S an Francisco's Downtown Crime District covers one of the oldest sections of the city. It includes old Yerba Buena. The area exemplifies the San Francisco tradition of evolution and has gone from being the entire city of San Francisco to a small section. The area was once the waterfront. Old maps of the city show how the waterline has been moved to reclaim land. There are still ships under the rubble, abandoned by sailors who sought fortune in the gold fields in the 1850's. It was easier to fill in around them than to demolish them. By the 1890's San Franciscans named the area in honor of the Barbary Coast in Africa where pirates spent their land time engaging in all manner of sin. The Barbary Coast Neighborhood in San Francisco was nine blocks of crime centered on Pacific Street, east of Stockton Street. After the Earthquake of 1906 it emerged like a Phoenix to be a major financial center of the west coast.

The crimes of Downtown reflect its various stages of development and include everything from fraud to homicide and bombings.

The Downtown District is bordered by Broadway to the north, the Embarcadero to the east, Market St. to the south, and Kearny to the west.

The Downtown Crime Scene Tour starts near the Cable Car turnaround at California St. and Market St. It ends at Kearny St. and Bush St.

1

1.1 101 California

101 California at Market St., 34th and 35th floors
Crime: Mass Murder
Scene Status: Remodeled, secure business

On July 1, 1993 a disgruntled former client rode up the elevator of 101 California. Gian Luigi Ferri got off at his former lawyers' offices suite occupying the 34th and 35th floors. He donned his hearing protection, and conducted a rampage shooting people with assault rifles. He killed eight, and wounded six before committing suicide.

Before the murders the shooter's businesses had failed. He seemed to target attorneys in the offices, but none of them were his actual attorneys who advised him on his business interests which had soured. It had been over a decade since he had dealings with the firm. The members of the firm he held grudges against had moved on.

California enacted tougher gun control laws including several against assault rifle after the event.

1.2 Fort Gunnybags

243 Sacramento Street, between Front and Davis Streets
Crime: Vigilantism
Scene Status: Destroyed by 1906 earthquake, new buildings

Fort Gunnybags is what the public called the Second Vigilance Committee headquarters. The building was a warehouse on the north side of Portsmouth Square, where blocks of commercial and residential buildings stand today. A gunny bag is a burlap bag used to ship agricultural products, and since San Francisco was having food shipped in, and little other than gold shipped out, there were a lot of those bags. Filled with sand, those bags became excellent fortification materials.

San Francisco's growth into a great city did not come without pain. Most people in San Francisco were focused on getting to the gold fields and making their fortune, the rest were intent on making their fortune on the first group. Plenty of people poured into San Francisco to leave rough circumstances back home. A portion of those folks brought their issues with them. Everyone rushed in, including ruffians who were interested in making money the old fashioned way, intimidation, graft, corruption, and theft. Murder was one of the messy tools employed. The early city paid little attention to laws. The good people of the city were under the law and behaved, while the lawless acted as they wished.

Casey shot King near the *Evening Bulletin* offices (see 1.8). The town had enough of the rampant lawlessness, the citizens rose up and took over the justice system. They founded the Second Committee of Vigilance. They held brief trials and hung their guilty. In 1856, the San Francisco Vigilance Committee made it their headquarters and arsenal and fortified it with gunnysacks. The Vigilance Committee erected gallows in Davis Street near Fort Gunnybags and executed Brace and Heatherington on July 29, 1856, for unrelated murders. The spot where the building stood is Landmark 90. It was built in 1856, and destroyed in the Earthquake of 1906.

1.3 Niantic

Sansome and Clay, Financial District
Crimes: Murder and Civil Rights
Scene Status: The ship is still buried there, but not visible

The Niantic was a ship turned into a building when San Franciscans filled in Yerba Buena Cove. A crew had sailed the Niantic to San Francisco and when the crew abandoned her to work the lucrative gold fields, she was stuck in the harbor. People being practical, they squatted on the Niantic and she became a warehouse and a place to live. She was also a hotel.

People engage in homicide, and they did it with alarming frequency in Gold Rush San Francisco. In 1861 a man robbed a store in the Niantic, and as he was running away, the woman who owned the store called him a thief. He did not care for the label, and returned the following day to express outrage. He shot the barber George W. Gordon in his chair. The Civil War was brewing back east, while men rushed into San Francisco with their ideas about whether California should be a free state or a slave state.

Robert Cowles witnessed the shooting from a barbershop. He also happened to be at least part African American. The debate became whether the man could testify or not, and physicians were called in to determine, "scientifically," whether he was African American or not. These physicians determined he was 1/16th African American and his ability to testify was ruled out. There was another witness who was able to testify and the murderer was found guilty.

People rose up to remove the restrictive law from the books, moving toward a more equal system of laws in California.

1.4 Shanghai Kelly's Boarding House and Tavern

33 Pacific St. East of Davis St. Calico Jim's Tavern nearby
Crime: Kidnapping, Human Trafficking
Scene Status: Most of Pacific Street was destroyed and rebuilt
after the earthquake

In Nineteenth Century San Francisco, the word *Shanghai* was used as a verb to describe kidnapping. Men who were Shanghaied to be forced into service as sailors. Several bars on the Barbary Coast lured men in for a drink, and drugged them. The men would then be delivered to a waiting ship's captain who would pay for them, and pass the bill on to them to work off. Many of the ships were bound for Shanghai, and thus the name stuck.

In the 1890's Shanghai Kelly made a living supplying labor to the ships in the form of kidnapped drugged men out of his boarding house and tavern at 33 Pacific Street with 3 trap doors in the bar. In the 1890's the area was still a shallow bay, with acres of docks, with bars on the docks. Consider the convenience of dropping a kidnapped person through a trap door into a boat to deliver him to a ship. Legend has it the kidnapper set an infamous record for mass kidnapping by holding a fake party on a Bay cruise. He drugged everyone on board, and delivered 90 men to his customers. Many have doubted the story, but it makes a good tale.

Calico Jim was one of Shanghai Kelly's contemporaries, and had a lot of the same nasty business habits. Criminals tend to be pragmatic and will keep doing what works, which was Jim's mistake. He was bad enough to get the attention of the local law enforcement;

a feat when the authorities ignored a lot of crime. The six different police men who went to arrest Calico Jim him over time all found themselves Shanghaied for their trouble. Imagine their surprise waking up on a slow boat headed across the Pacific. The men all made it back to SF after their round trips. Legend has it they pooled their resources to fund the hunt for Calico Jim. They located him in Callao Peru, South America and sent a killer to avenge the crimes.

1.5 The Hippodrome

555 Pacific Ave. near Montgomery
Crimes: Prostitution and Alcohol
Scene Status: Building still there, new occupants

When today's Financial District was the Barbary Coast the Hippodrome stood out as an extreme version of a wicked den of sin on Pacific St. The wickedest street in San Francisco. The club was just one of many businesses catering to nearly every vice and included rooms for customers to live them out. It was a bright example of the wild living many of San Francisco's more conservative public wished to stamp out. The club's last location in the 1920's was 555 Pacific. It occupied other locations on the street including 560 Pacific, which is no longer standing.

The 1906 Earthquake, the local populace revolting against corruption of city hall in the same era, and the California Red Light Abatement Act all worked in concert to clean up the area.

Now the area houses office buildings, pubs, and stores. The Hippodrome is an art store.

1.6 Lucas, Turner and Company Bank Offices

800 Montgomery St. at Jackson St. northeast corner
Crime: Prefame Location, Celebrity
Scene Status: Building still there, with modifications

Most people know William Tecumseh Sherman as the Union General who broke the South in the US Civil War with his *March to the Sea* from Atlanta to Savannah. He burned a swath through the South and destroyed everything in his path with his doctrine of Scorched Earth. That makes him a hero to some and a war criminal to others.

In the 1850's Sherman was out of the Army, and cooling his heels in the city by the Bay. He was a bank manager at Lucas, Turner and Company Bank offices at the northeast corner of Montgomery St. and Jackson St. Sherman missed the 1851 Committee of Vigilance, but he was in San Francisco for the Second Committed of Vigilance when it started up. In 1856 he got involved when California's Governor appointed him Major General of the California Militia. He ended up walking a narrow line to keep order. His controlled actions prevented a civil war while allowing reestablishment of order.

In 1857 Sherman left California. In a few years he would be a famous man.

1.7 Belli Building

722 Montgomery Street Between Washington and Jackson
Crimes: Celebrity
Scene Status: Remodeled

Many people know who Melvin Belli was, without knowing his name. Melvin "King of Torts" Belli, was the lawyer who hosted a show on the radio for the Zodiac Killer to call in. Belli sued the SF Giants because the weather was too cold at the stadium. As a criminal and civil attorney, he represented Errol Flynn, Lenny Bruce, Mae West, Sirhan Sirhan, the Rolling Stones and Jack Ruby. Mr. Belli's book, *Modern Trials*, advocated the use of demonstrative evidence to win lawsuits.

The building was raised in 1849 or 1850 and destroyed by fire in 1851, and then rebuilt with the old walls and foundations. It is one of the oldest buildings in the city. The construction reflects the technology of the era with planks, six to eight inches thick and to a depth of eight feet laid as a foundation in the mud. In 1851 the city had just filled in Yerba Buena Cove, and there were hundreds of abandoned ships littered the harbor with wood to be harvested since they occupants were all in the hills seeking their fortune in gold.

Belli died bankrupt in July, 1996, leaving behind hundreds of unfinished cases worth millions to his clients and their lawyers.

1.8 The Evening Bulletin Offices

700 block of Montgomery (west side of street) , north of Washington
Crime: Murder
Scene Status: The building has been replaced. The streets still exist

In 1851, the citizens of San Francisco rose up and formed the First Committee of Vigilance to address the rampant crime problem compounded by corruption. The city went from under a thousand people to twenty thousand in three years with the Gold Rush, and plenty of problems flowed in with the people. The 1851 Committee of Vigilance hung eight people through summary trials, and banished fourteen. After three months the leaders returned power to the local government.

Five years passed, and the citizens grew restless with what they saw as a deterioration of civility. The catalyst for the Second Vigilance Committee came in the form of another feud between two men. Mass communication feuds were not invented with the internet. James King of William (1822-1856), was a banker business man. On October 8, 1855, he started the publication of the *Evening Bulletin* which contained 4 pages, 10 by 15 inches.

King of William's rival was James Casey who was the target of nasty articles in the Bulletin. Casey's predictable response was to begin his own paper, The Sunday Times. The two began a newspaper feud, although King's paper did most of the fighting.

King used his paper to skewer immorality and corruption in San Francisco. He had served with the 1851 Committee of Vigilance. He had experience with the process and acted as foreman of the grand jury which indicted the City Treasurer in November of 1853.

Casey's paper, the *Sunday Times*, targeted Thomas King (James's brother) who was vying for a position in the custom house. The response by the King side was to search Casey's background in New York, prior to coming to San Francisco.

The boiling point came when King's side used the information they had discovered in New York: Casey had been arrested and convicted of a felony. Other newspapers passed on publication. King did not. There were court documents, and Sing Sing Prison was a famous place.

May 14, 1856, Casey visited King in his office at the Bulletin's editorial room, on the Merchant and Montgomery Streets. He asked him not to publish the story about him. King listened to his argument, with pistol in hand, and then told him to leave. Casey theorized one of the two would fall as a result of publishing the information. The same day the *Bulletin* published the Casey record, and at the end of the day, Casey confronted King on the West side of Montgomery, north of Washington. He told King to draw and defend himself. King continued walking, and Casey shot him. Casey shot him in the chest. He was carried to a room in the Montgomery Block which is now the site of the Transamerica Pyramid. Six days later, King died, and the authorities arrested Casey.

Casey was taken to city prison on Kearny Street. Casey is said to have sought the safety of the jail rather than be free.

The public's patience ran out with the lawlessness, and so started the Second Vigilance Committee.

The incident incited the public. The Second Vigilance Committee swelled in number to 8,000 members. The Committee hanged Casey the same day as King's funeral, May 22, 1856 at 243 Sacramento Street, Fort Gunnybags (see 1.2).

1.9 Bubble Lounge

700 Block of Montgomery Street, near Washington
Crime: Murder
Scene Status: The lounge closed in 2015, building still there

Everyone has a nightmare of being picked up in a cab, and never being seen alive again. In 1999 San Francisco was having the new Gold Rush fueled by the Dot.com money. On May 14, 1999 a 24 year old office worker Julie Day went out to party and never came home. She was partying at the Bubble Lounge Bar and told by the manager she could not smoke inside. Given the choice between leaving and staying and not smoking she caught a cab alone.

A week later her body was located at a construction site near what is today the baseball stadium. The medical examiner ruled she had been asphyxiated. The police investigation led to her cab driver Jehad Baqleh. The courts convicted him and sent him to a mental hospital due to insanity.

1.10 Transamerica Pyramid

600 Montgomery St. near Clay St. 41st Floor
Crime: Fraud
Scene Status: The overall scene is still there, secured building

The Transamerica Pyramid is the second most recognizable iconic structure in San Francisco. It is also one of the most unpredictable scenes to be attached to a crime. The building was erected in 1972 after vicious opposition.

In the early 1990's the Soviet Union had remarketed itself as the Russian Federation, and with its rush toward privatization it sold off state assets including diamonds. Golden ADA was a diamond polisher in business on the 41st floor of the Pyramid in 1992-1993. They later moved to the Jewelry Mart at 999 Brannan.

When it was all over, $130,000,000 to $170,000,000 was unaccounted for. The case included suicides and jailings on multiple continents. The main man of the ADA Group was Andrei Kozlenok. The last new report of him was his extradition from Athens to Moscow.

1.11 Diamond Hoax of 1872

Financial District
Crime: Fraud
Scene Status: The overall scene has been changed

The diamond case involving the Transamerica Pyramid was not the first one time San Francisco had crime involving diamonds. In the latter half of the 19th century, San Francisco was a town built on the mines of the Sierras. There was commerce in the Fog City, but the big money came from the ground, and everybody wanted a piece of it. Greed facilitates confidence games and Asbury Harpending and his friends knew it. Harpending was no stranger to fantastic San Francisco crime (see 1.18) as he previously ran a caper to hijack gold during the Civil War.

The con men sowed a mine in the mountains with industrial diamonds and set the trap in San Francisco by going to visit local businessman George D. Roberts at his office and try to swear him to secrecy. The request for secrecy which usually causes people to share, and greed only caused a spread of the news and stoked the fires. Investors flocked to them, setting up a corporation, called The San Francisco and New York Mining and Commercial Co. Geologist Charles King was dubious, and visited the site, determining it was worthless, thus shutting down the plot in its early phases.

The other players include Ralston who would build the Palace Hotel at the corner of Market and New Montgomery.

1.12 Armed Forces Police HQ

Clay Street, between Montgomery and Kearny
Crime: Bombing, Terror, Social Cause
Scene Status: The Chinese Education Center now occupies the building

San Francisco has had a lot of bombings for a lot of different causes. On July 28, 1970 a bomb attack was conducted on the Armed Forces Police Headquarters in San Francisco. The offices were located in a two story building to the west of the Hotel Justice, and east of the Royal Hotel.

The alleged bombers were interested in violence to bring the war to America. The cause was to protest bombing North Vietnam. They fashioned a simple pipe bomb and exploded it in the trash bin, causing damage, but not injuring anyone. According to an anonymous interview, the bomb was exploded in Merchant Alley, which was on the back side of the office.

The Department of Defense put the AFPHQ in downtown San Francisco, on the other side of town from the Presidio Army

Base because most of the troops were interested in having a San Francisco, "experience," in the bars and clubs, and the police were going where the business was. Up until 1968 the Hall of Justice was on Portsmouth Square, where the Holiday Inn tower stands today, so there was a connection to civilian law enforcement.

There is no record of anyone being arrested for the crime.

1.13 American Exchange Hotel

Sansome and Halleck, plus San Francisco Bay
Crime: Treason and Robbery
Scene Status: The Bay and streets remain, but the water line used to be near the base of the slope

San Francisco was not a part of any of the great battles of the American Civil War, but San Francisco did have adventurers from both sides of the conflict who brought their beliefs with them when they came. The gold from California helped finance the Union effort to the tune of a million dollars a week towards the end of the war. San Francisco was involved in the conflict, pleasing some and offending others. The gold made the trip south along the coast, and rounded the southern tip of South America and then went north to deliver the shipment, or over the Isthmus of Panama. Either way, it was a tough trip. In the meantime, the concept of a Transcontinental Railroad was moving forward, but not complete.

In the Spring of 1863, a few San Francisco based Southern sympathizers decided to go into the privateer business, and use a fast ship to do it. Asbury Harpending was the brains behind the outfit. Less than a decade later he would be a key player in the Great Diamond Hoax. Harpending said Jefferson Davis, President of the

Confederate States of America, had approved of his plan to be a pirate, and take California for the South. Harpending planned to capture Union ships with California gold. He hired a William C. Law as a captain, and with Ridgeley Greathouse bought the ship, the *J. M. Chapman* for the purpose of turning her into a privateer and take over gold ships. The men outfitted the ship with cannon. They prepared to sail on March 15, 1863.

On the evening of March 14, 1863, the men met in an alley way behind the American Exchange Hotel. They then left for the ship. Today, the area is covered by 335 Sansome, a large office building. Halleck St. runs to the north of the building. Today's Halleck looks like an alley, and the conspirators walked either down Halleck St. or California St. toward the waterfront.

Secret plans have a way of losing their secrecy in taverns, and Isaiah Lees, San Francisco's great detective of the era, was involved in thwarting the plot through his informants. Lees and his men watched the ship load up and prepare to leave the harbor on the evening of March 14, 1863. The ship was boarded by sailors of the *USS Cyane* and all were arrested. The arrestors were the federal revenue officers, the US Navy, and the San Francisco Police. Investigators found all the men, and their arms marked as, "machinery." Several of men were charged with treason, and housed at Alcatraz Island to await trial. They posted bail, and went back to their games.

1.14 Ralston's Bank

Northwest corner of California and Sansome streets and the Sub Treasury on Montgomery between Sacramento and Sansome
Crime: Fraud, Unauthorized exchange of gold
Scene Status: New Buildings

In July 1869 Ralston's Bank of California was like a lot of banks in the area. It had a lot of gold, and was involved in the mining and railroad industries. America's President Ulysses S Grant shut off the exchange of gold to minted coin for a brief period while getting settled in office. The rule was fine for east coast banks, but for San Francisco it could have been disastrous.

William Ralston's Bank of California had loaned to the railroads, and although he had gold, it was not in coin. Ralston's Bank had a liquidity problem. He recognized the potential panic, with the citizens having concerns about being able to get their money out of the bank.

Financial crimes like fraud can come off as greyer than those of violence. The legend has no mention of the possibility of paying depositors back with gold rather than coin. Ralston engineered the solution to exchange his bank's gold for coin under cover of darkness. Maurice Dore, and Asbury Harpending shuttled what they estimated to be five tons of gold between the bank and the Sub Treasury.

The following morning the Bank of California opened and the customers were happy to see there was plenty of coin available for them, and the bank was solid. There was no run on the bank. There was also no story of any charges filed for the late night exchange. Six years later Ralston's bank failed anyhow. (see 3.6).

1.15 Pioneer Loan and Savings Bank

Montgomery and California Streets
Crime: Fraud
Scene Status: New Buildings

Joseph C. Duncan started Pioneer Loan and Savings Bank in San Francisco, in 1875. Many called it J. C. Duncan's Bank. Duncan hit upon the idea to have feeder banks, which sounds a lot like shell companies. Two of them were, "Fidelity" and "Union." Both of those institutions failed and have no relation to any modern banks with the same names. Conglomerates coupled with moving money around, and having dummy directors and divisions becoming insolvent creates for problems. He also became known for paying higher interest rates to attract customers. His bank returned 12% compared to his competitors who returned 8%.

On October 8, 1877 bank failed. The failure amount was $1.2 million dollars One version of the audit listed the forgeries as $800,000 with the loss of over $1,000,000 spread among 2000 plus depositors.

Duncan's bank was near Ralston's Bank of California. The small community of bankers would have made him aware of the outcome of the Bank of California's troubles for Ralston. Faced with a series of unpleasant options, Duncan chose to flee. The famous Detective Captain Isiah Lees investigated the case. Duncan gave the detective the slip . for a little while. On February 24, 1878, the detectives found him at a dressmaker's parlor at 509 Kearny, at California, which was up the hill from the bank. He had a hiding place in a fake bureau.

Duncan was charged with forgery, embezzlement, and theft. His wife divorced him. He was tried yet never convicted. A free man, he died in a shipwreck some twenty years after.

1.16 Black Bart Home

420 Montgomery St. at California St.
Crime: Robbery
Scene Status: Wells Fargo Museum

Black Bart is one of the most famous robbers in American History. Charles E. Boles was his original name, and then he took up Charles E. Bolton. The public named him Black Bart. He supposedly fought in the Civil War and came west to work in Northern California, settling in San Francisco. In the city he became a man about town who wore nice clothes and projected an air of culture. Culture takes money and learned how to get it. He robbed stagecoaches, but he stood out as a gentleman and had a reputation for being courteous, chivalrous, and for never hurting anyone in the process of relieving the stage coach of its strongbox. Black Bart also was a poet who went by, "P o 8."

There were 29 Wells Fargo Stagecoach robberies attributed to Black Bart. Starting in July 26, 1875, and ending November 3, 1883. Wells Fargo had a lower opinion of the robber than the public did, and they got Pinkerton's detectives involved, to hunt down the man who had cost them a lot of money. Wells Fargo Museum's address is the scene, because it has the greatest repository of Black Bart information.

The police of the time had limited ways to track a person, and most of them involved a lot of work, and contact with people to develop leads. The undoing of the skilled robber was losing his handkerchief at a scene.

Detective James Hume followed up on leads, and ran into Bart downtown, and brought him to the Wells Fargo bank on November 12, 1883. Their interview went late into the night, and Hume, Bolton, and SFPD Captain Stone went to Bolton's residence where they located evidence connecting the handkerchief from the scene to additional laundry marked, "F.X.O.7"

Detectives found poetry left at the scene considered to be of the same author as the poetry at an earlier scene. Bart got a short sentence and after five years was set free. Upon release, a member of the press asked him if he would re-offend. He said he would not. Another asked if he would write any more poetry, and he responded by asking the reporter whether his previous response was heard.

The Wells Fargo museum now occupies the location, so you can see more about Black Bart there.

1.17 Chronicle Offices

420 Montgomery St. at California St.
Crime: Celebrity and Murder
Scene Status: No longer there

Public feuds have been a part of San Francisco life from the beginning. In 1880 a feud between the mayor and a newspaper publisher boiled over.

DeYoung responded first at the Old Mint by shooting Isaac Smith Kalloch at the Old Mint (see 5.7). Time passed, and Kalloch won the election. DeYoung awaited his trial on attempted murder charges. On April 23,1880 DeYoung visited the *Chronicle* offices in the evening. Isaac Kalloch's son Isaac M. ambushed DeYoung and shot him in his office, hitting him one time in the mouth. The bullet struck the newspaper man's veins in his neck and he died.

The younger Kalloch was tried for murder and acquitted.

2. Chinatown and North Beach

The Chinatown and North Beach Crime District shows two old and unique neighborhoods. They are ethnic districts where the people in them retain their culture in the greater melting pot of the city.

Chinatown is one of the oldest settled parts of the city. The Chinese started coming to San Francisco in the 1840's and built Chinatown. When they started, Grant St. was called Dupont, and Chinatown was the edge of town. Chinatown history is filled with a vibrant culture thriving in the face of adversity and sometimes open hostility. Over the years it has been burned down, damaged by earthquakes, and attacked by mobs of angry workers.

North Beach started also as a scrub and sand dune filled landscape on the north side of town. It was an area known for its fishermen's cottages. One of its earliest plans for development coincided with a massive fraud. Land developers planned to fill housing needs along with their own pockets. Italian immigrants gravitated to the area, and developed its culture seen today. Along the way in the 1950's the area was center to the Beat Generation.

The crimes of Chinatown and North Beach do not always represent nor are they the cause of the ethnic communities. Some crimes include homicide, bombings, drugs, and prostitution.

Chinatown centers on Grant Ave. starting south from Bush St to Broadway in the north. Chinatown covers two blocks on each side of Grant Ave. North Beach starts within a block of Broadway and goes north to Fisherman's Wharf. It goes a few blocks west of Columbus St. It is bordered on the east by the Embarcadero.

The Chinatown and North Beach Crime Scene Tour starts at the south end of Chinatown at the Dragon's Gate at Grant Ave. and Bush St. It ends in North Beach near Grant Ave. at Chestnut St.

2.1 814 California Apartments

First floor, 814 California St. at Stockton St.
Crime: Murder
Scene Status: The apartment building is still there

Mrs. Rosetta Baker was a wealthy woman who had a talent for real estate, and a taste for young men. At 65 her romantic interest was a 28 year old actor named Walter Franklin Outler, or Middleton as his stage name. December 7, 1930 was another cold winter night in the city. Mrs. Baker's friend named Mrs. Graves dated Outler's 23 year old pianist roommate. The two couples had a double date. At the end of it, the two men left with Mrs. Baker.

The following morning Mrs. Baker was found dead, and robbed of her ring, as well as assaulted. Evidence indicated the suspect fought with Mrs. Baker.

Liu Fook was a 62 year old housekeeper for Mrs. Baker, and had been at it for 9 years. Fook told investigators he saw the victim embracing Middleton. Baker fired Fook multiple times in the past. In a case filled with oddities, Fook's personal habit of requesting he be able to smoke his daily opium pipe did him no favors. He became the prime suspect. A search of Fook's apartment at 841 Stockton revealed no evidence to connect him to the crime. The trial wound its way and in March, Fook was found not guilty after a short deliberation. Fook left for China afterward, and was not heard from again.

Mrs. Baker continued to shock her family from the grave as her will excluded much of them. She gave her wealth to her niece in LA.

Middleton became a Hollywood actor and talent agent. He died on December 7, 1960. His only film listed on the film websites is, *An American Tragedy* from 1931. It is a love story between a poor man and wealthy woman complicated by pregnancy.

2.2 Chinatown Rescue

The Donaldina Cameron House, 950 Sacramento at Joice Alley
Crimes: Human Trafficking, Prostitution, and Death
Scene Status: Chinatown was rebuilt after the 1906 Earthquake, and there is a rebuilt house dedicated to the same cause on the location

The Donaldina Cameron House was a rescue home for prostitutes ran by Ms. Cameron. Back in the 1800's and into the twentieth century, prostitution was rampant in the city and Ms. Cameron set herself on a course to eradicate it. She went on raids of houses of prostitution and created a home for the women and girls who escaped the life.

Ms. Cameron was a New Zealand immigrant who brought her religious views into her fight against the exploitation of Chinese girls and women. There was a significant amount of graft in the city, the challenges of closing down such enterprises were even greater.

Ms. Cameron must have learned a few tricks from dealing with the wily adversaries. The basement of her building had a number of hiding places for girls who had been rescued, and wanted to prevent being returned to their abusers. Tragedy struck the movement after the 1906 earthquake when a fire burned the rescue home. Evacuation would have been the right choice, but out of fear or ignorance, the women and girls stayed and many were killed who could have fled. Today, the building is brick, and houses a school. The organization has merged with others and still operates as a shelter and provider of social services in the Bay Area and beyond.

2.3 Dupont and Clay

Southeast corner of Dupont (Present day Grant) and Clay
Crimes: Murder
Scene Status: There are new buildings

On July 7, 1865, a man who escaped the Vigilantes from the 1850's wreaked havoc from his room in Chinatown. Billy Mulligan started in New York, and came to San Francisco for the Gold Rush. He involved himself in local politics, and even worked in the jails as a keeper. He was concerned enough by the Vigilantes and their actions to leave San Francisco, and return to New York. After killing a man, and spending a little time in prison, he returned to Fog City in 1864.

Mulligan suffered from delirium tremens and thought the Vigilantes were after him. His rented room in the hotel overlooked the street, and he shot and wounded a Chinese laundryman across the street. His friend John McNabb sought to help him with a whisky and Mulligan shot and killed him for his efforts. Mulligan then shot and killed firefighter John Hart.

Officers then took up positions surrounding the shooter. When he showed himself, Officer Hopkins shot and killed him.

2.4 Little Pete's Barber

821 Washington Street at Waverly
Crime: Murder and Organized Crime
Scene Status: New Buildings

Fong Ching AKA Little Pete lived fast and died young in Chinatown during the 1880's and 90's. Little Pete was in many ways an American success story. He immigrated, learned the culture of the new country, and prospered. He was born in Canton China around 1864 and came to San Francisco at 10 years old. He went to Sunday School at the Methodist Chinese Mission and spoke fluent English and became an interpreter to many business affairs. He learned about the shoe trade and opened a factory under the name, F. C. Peters & Co. which allowed him to deal in shoes to a public not always welcoming to Chinese business owners. Like the mafia dons of the movies, he had family with wife and children.

Little Pete established a true organized crime organization, referred to as a tong. Little Pete had the reputation as being the smartest among smart people. His skills and success made him a target. The men who dispensed violence were called, "hatchet men," because they used a lathe operator's hatchet to assault people in the course of their business. Another term for them was, "highbinders," courtesy of the New York City Police.

On October 28, 1886 Little Pete's bodyguard Lee Chuck shot and killed a rival at the corner of Washington St. and Spofford Alley. SFPD Officer J. B. Martin apprehended him, and during apprehension Chuck pulled his gun on the officer. Little Pete attempted to bribe the officer for $400 to lie about the incident. Little Pete was indicted. After allegations of bribed jurors, Little Pete got five years in Folsom for a sentence.

Little Pete served his time and after prison he turned his attention to the Bay District Track. He gambled on horses, winning an estimated $100.000 in a few weeks during 1896. Naturally, the track owners barred him. The Bay District Track was located on the north side of Golden Gate Park, between First and Fifth Avenues, and Fulton Street to Point Lobos Rd, which is now Geary. It operated 1874 to 1896. Little Pete ran the lotteries, gambling, horse racing, fan tan rooms, extortion, protection rackets, prostitution, and drug dens.

On the evening of January 24, 1897 Little Pete left his home upstairs in the building at 821 Washington St. He went downstairs to the barbershop. His body guard Ed Murray left the shop to pick up a copy of a newspaper for the latest horse race results. Little Pete had a contract on his life. Two men ran into the shop and fired pistols at close range killing the man. The account said they ran from the scene, and into Waverly Place around the corner. An opulent funeral followed, including an American Military Band leading the parade.

2.5 The Golden Dragon Restaurant

816 Washington Street at Waverly
Crime: Murder and Organized Crime
Scene Status: Now Imperial Palace Chinatown

The Golden Dragon Restaurant was like a lot of nice places to get a late night dinner. On September 4, 1977 at 2:00 AM the shooting started in the dining room, and after about a minute five people were killed and 11 wounded in what was termed by the media as a gang war. There were no confirmed injuries or deaths of gang members.

Less than 10 years before the Chinatown Squad was disbanded after the public branded it a racist holdover from Gold Rush San Francisco. The incident also led to an Asian Crime Task Force, to restart the lapsed enforcement. The trial indicated the massacre was the result of a gang turf war, and several members of the shooting team went to prison.

2.6 St. Louis Alley

Off Jackson St. west of Grant
Crime: Drugs
Scene Status: Renewed

The historical crime in Chinatown included the alleys. Even today, they have an air of mystery about them. A historical crime scene in general has an energy, but a gloomy alleyways always seems like a canyon.

In the 1870's race relations between whites and Chinese in San Francisco were at a low. The city's government enacted and enforced a series of laws to go after Chinese culture. They started with a map of Chinatown showing every occupant and its connection to drugs, prostitution, religious houses, and gambling. The map had dozens of examples of each, but an easy place to see is St. Louis Alley. Halfway down the alley as one enters from Jackson St. there was an opium place of manufacture and then a resort for customers to come and smoke the drug.

2.7 Chinatown Race Riots

Chinatown
Crime: Arson, Murder, Social Cause, Terror
Scene Status: Chinatown was rebuilt after the 1906
Earthquake

Political parties could morph into mobs, and the reverse is true also. San Francisco was an immigrant town for a lot of its early times, and those people often brought their ideas with them including organized labor. In the 1850's to 1860's the Gold Rush brought about a strong economy with people making large amounts of money. The railroads caused financial and social upheaval when the owners employed thousands of Chinese workers to build the tracks connecting the east to the west of America.

Most of the Chinese workers on the railroads were paid far less than their European counterparts. Cheap labor benefited companies, but led to a labor crisis.

In 1873, the Workingmen's Party was a Socialist party founded by whites and included an anti-Chinese platform. The party's other name was the Socialist Labor Party of America. It had a strong appeal to a lot of unemployed workmen who felt they were being undercut by a labor pool which stayed after their contact was up. The party won municipal elections and got Mayor Andrew Bryant elected to mayor. Bryant Street is named after him. Bryant created all sorts of stricter laws for the Chinese in particular, including a 2:00 AM curfew. The Workingmen's Mayor was also the one who ushered in the Nation's first anti-drug law by making it a misdemeanor to keep or visit an opium den. Medicinal use (by whites) was still ok.

On July 23, 1877 the economy was bad and it fanned the flames of anger for out of work men. The Workingmen's Party held a rally on the sandlots near the City Hall, which is the present day Civic Center. James D'Arcy organized a 5000-8000 person strong mob on Market St, and they marched to Chinatown. Once they arrived, they looted, and burned. They even sabotaged the firemen's hoses, but cutting them to prevent extinguishment. The mayor was concerned enough to call for federal aid, and two warships arrived to the waterfront. The *USS Pensacola* and the *USS Lancaster* stayed out of the fight, never deploying troops. Four people were killed. The violence continued for a day, and was only stopped when the police, state militia, and the citizen's vigilance committee teamed up to stop it.

2.8 The Sentinel Building

916 Kearny St. at Columbus Ave.
Crimes: Corruption, Organized Crime
Scene Status: The overall scene is still there, with modifications

San Francisco has gone through its share of political crimes and that includes political boss and fixer Abe Ruef. Ruef was a local, born in the city in 1864. He went to college at the University of California across the Bay and studied criminal justice since he wanted to clean up a corrupt San Francisco. He graduated at 18 and then studied law and passed the Bar at 21. He also spoke eight languages. He got into politics and even formed his own political party, the Union Labor Party in 1901.

Ruef backed Mayor Eugene Schmitz for mayor, and he won in 1902. Schmitz 's previous job was band leader. While he lacked credentials to be a mayor, he also lacked any scandals. Schmitz became the face of San Francisco leadership, Ruef worked the levers of power behind the scenes from his office in the Sentinel Building.

The reform movement took hold in the city, and many prominent citizens began to push to clean up city Hall, and address the rampant problems so obvious in the Barbary Coast. The 1906 Earthquake hit and destroyed City Hall in under a few minutes. It also destroyed the network of corruption and soon most of the city's government was facing a trial for corruption. Ruef got a sentence of 14 years for bribery and was released from prison in 1915, and died bankrupt.

The building is still there, and has a beautiful oxidized copper green. It is also where Francis Ford Coppola has his offices.

2.9 San Francisco Brewing Company

155 Columbus Ave. at Pacific Ave.
Crimes: Fugitive, Celebrity, Drugs and Alcohol
Scene Status: The overall scene is still there, with modifications other names for the tavern now called the Comstock Saloon

San Francisco has a long and proud history of being a bar town, at times the ratio of bars to people exceeded the ratio of churches to people. The tavern started in 1907 as the Andromeda Saloon, it went through a few name changes, and by 1985 it was named the San Francisco Brewing Company. As of 2010 it was renamed the Comstock Saloon, but in 2012 it started using the San Francisco Brewing Company name for its beers again.

Baby Face Nelson was born 1908 as Lester Joseph Gillis. He died 1934 in a shootout with the FBI. He held the distinction of being responsible for the deaths of three agents, a record.

According to local lore, Baby Face Nelson spent a lot of time in the bar. Nelson is thought of as a Chicago gangster, but he did plenty of underground work out in San Francisco during Prohibition. The FBI bio on him does not refer to the San Francisco Brewing Company, but mostly of his crime exploits back east. Several accounts describe him as being captured in the basement restroom of the tavern during the late 1920's or early 1930's.

2.10 City Lights Bookstore

261 Columbus Avenue near Broadway
Crime: Art, Obscenity, Celebrity, Civil Rights
Scene Status: Still there

The City Lights Bookstore is famous the world over for being a great bookstore on its own and its association with the Beat Generation. The bookstore was established in 1953 by a WWII veteran and PhD. from Columbia, Dr. Lawrence Ferlinghetti. His background indicated a traditional individual who would maintain the status quo. The reverse is more the case.

Ferlinghetti made his way west, and established the bookstore, and publishing house at City Lights. He was a fixture in North Beach. Other stars of the constellation were Kerouac, and Burroughs. When Ginsberg read *Howl* read at the Six Gallery on October 7, 1955, it would go on to be credited as the first event of the Beat Generation. On March 25, 1957 Ferlinghetti along with his manager Shigoyeshi Murao were arrested by the US Police and

Customs agents on obscenity charges for his role in publishing Ginsberg's *Howl*. A subsequent trial resulted in Judge Clayton Horn ruling the poem had redeeming social value, which meant it was not obscene – even if people found it obscene.

2.11 Condor Club

300 Columbus at Broadway
Crimes: Death, Obscenity, and Celebrity
Scene Status: The overall scene is still there

San Francisco has a long and colorful history with sex, and its interaction with the law. San Francisco is a place where the obscenity laws seem to have their showdowns, whether the Barbary Coast of a century ago, bathhouses in the 1980's, or the recent controversies surrounding a BDSM facility.

The Condor Club is a long time San Francisco entertainment venue. Its marquee is shown in a lot of movies and TV shows taking place in the city. The most famous person associated with it is the Carol Doda. There is a plaque out front commemorating the day in 1964 when she performed her full nude show. In 1965 Carol Doda and club manager Gino Del Preto were arrested for lewdness. The case wound down and San Francisco allowed nude dancing. Carol Doda retired from the trade, but held onto her position as a cultural icon in the city. She passed in a nursing home in 2015.

The Condor Club prided itself on its creative shows. One number included lowering a piano from the ceiling. On November 23, 1983 an assistant manager (or bouncer depending on accounts) and a dancer decided they would make their own after hours show on the famous piano. During the act one of the participants activated the switch to raise the piano. The equipment either suffered a failure or had no safety features. The two spent the night pinned between the piano and the ceiling. The janitor discovered them when he arrived the following morning and called 911. When it was over, the bouncer was dead from being crushed.

2.12 Café Trieste

601 Vallejo at Grant
Crime: Celebrity, Art, and Social Change, No actual Crime
Scene Status: same as ever

Café Trieste is a great coffeehouse. It was opened in 1956, in time to be a major meeting place for the Beats as they thrived in North Beach. Some called members of the Beat Generation Beatniks. The café is not an actual crime scene, but its connection the coffee shop has with crime comes with a great movie about crime. Rumors say Francis Ford Coppola adapted his screenplay of the *Godfather* at the tables there. A lot of authors have got their coffee there. It is up the block and around the corner from City Lights Bookstore. The structure is still there, and it has had the occasional remodel, but it feels like an old place.

2.13 Green St.

Green St. runs east west from the Embarcadero to the
Presidio
Crime: Fugitive
Scene Status: The street changes

In the early days of American San Francisco, the city was wide
open for anyone, and there were few restrictions since it was the far
side of the world, with a lot of distance between SF and anyone who
could enforce it.

Paul Geddes changed his name to Talbot Green when he came
west in 1841. He spent time in Monterey, and in 1844 settled in San
Francisco. He became a prosperous merchant, and famous in the
city, rising to Customs Collection, and an arbitrator for disputes.
Along the way, the city was closer to changing from Mexican
territory to US territory, and he became a favorite candidate for
Mayor, which he turned down. He also shunned a senatorial spot,
which would have meant big power and a lucrative payoff from
lobbyists. In 1849 when the city was being surveyed, Green Street
was named after him. The street runs east west through most of the
city.

The unravelling came in October 1850 when the city was
having its parade to celebrate its admission to the Union. Green led
the parade, and whatever anonymity he had in San Francisco was
shattered. A woman shared her story with a newspaper claiming
Green was a false identity for Paul Geddes from Pennsylvania.
Before he left the Keystone state, he had been carrying his
employer's funds when he decided to gamble with. He lost his
employer's money. His solution was to leave his wife and five
children and come west.

Green denied all charges and demanded a retraction from the newspaper. His friends supported him, up until the time he admitted it. His follow up act was to ship out to Panama. He returned the city years later to try and rebuild, but those who knew him shunned him. The story goes he returned to his wife. The street name remains.

2.14 Coit Tower

Monument to Lillie Coit, Telegraph Hill Blvd. from Lombard St.
Crime: Celebrity and Treason
Scene Status: The overall scene is still there, with modifications

Lillie Coit was an original San Francisco Bad Girl, and Good Girl. As a child she helped a Fire Brigade, and as a wealthy benefactor she continued to provide assistance to those organizations. She had a reputation for hanging out in bars, and smoking cigars. While tame by today's standards, it was scandalous in the nineteenth century.

Ms. Coit was also a Southern Sympathizer, and is reported to have helped at least one Rebel get out of town. In her brush with treason she spent part of the Civil War in France translating documents between the Confederate States of America and France.

Ms. Coit left a third of her estate to the City of San Francisco. The city used the money was to build Coit Tower. Diego Rivera fans will be happy to know he painted murals in the monument as one of the 26 artists hired by the Works Progress Administration.

2.15 Telegraph Hill Quarry

Green and Sansome
Crimes: Nuisance and Murder
Scene Status: The overall scene is still there, with modifications, and vegetation overgrow

Telegraph hill is another marvelous oddity in San Francisco connected with crime. The hill is a high natural feature near downtown, and visible from a lot of the city. Before radio, the hill served as a semaphore station to receive visual signals from incoming ships in the Bay. The hill is also accentuated by Coit Tower, and looks down on North Beach to its west.

The east side of the hill is the crime history part from the 1890's. The back side looks down on the piers. It is exposed rock from years of blasting away at a quarry. The quarry in the middle of the city was used to mine rocks for building materials and ship ballasts.

The quarry was one of many in the area run by two brothers, George and Harry Gray. People in the area complained about the two who insisted on operating long after it was clear the rest of the city was tired of blasting, along with the danger to them and their property. The 1890's were the decade in the run up to the corruption scandal exposed right after the Earthquake of 1906, so perhaps politicians, and their underlings were tolerant of their blatant disregard for the law, and decency.

The two Grays were never held accountable for the dangers and property losses. But Harry was held accountable in another way. On November 10, 1914 when a worker named Joe Lococco who worked at the other family owned quarry at 29th and Castro went to collect his backpay of $17.50. George refused him. Lococco shot him dead. The court found the shooter Joe not guilty by temporary insanity, and released him afterward.

2.16 Saints Peter and Paul Church

Washington Square, 666 Filbert St. at Powell
Crime: Bombing and Terror
Scene Status: same as ever

Saints Peter and Paul Church in North Beach is famous for being a grand church, close to a cathedral. It is reminder of the Italian Catholic roots in the neighborhood. The faith survived the Beats, Hippies, and sex shows nearby. It is a massive and beautiful building most people associate with Joe DiMaggio and Marilyn Monroe's wedding. They got married at City Hall, while the public received the photos from the Church.

There were five bombings at Saints Peter and Paul Church from 1926 and 1927. No people were hurt, but the message was one of anger, violence and intimidation. The bombings came to an end on March 6, 1927 when police foiled the plan by shooting the two would be bombers as they were getting ready to bomb the church again. They had 26 sticks of explosive ready to light. One man was killed, reports identify him only as Ricca. The other man was Celesten Eklund, who was injured and later died without providing any information. Eklund was an anarchist who had given public speeches on the subject. There were no more bombings of the church after their deaths.

2.17 Alleged Government Brothel

225 Chestnut St. near Grant Ave.
Crime: Prostitution and Drugs
Scene Status: Remodeled, beautiful views

The Internet, home to conspiracy theories, held there was a CIA sponsored brothel in San Francisco where the Johns were dosed with LSD during their visits. The newspaper said it was called, "Operation Midnight Climax." The research project was run from 1955 to 1965. The story goes the man who ran it retired across the bay to become the Fire Marshall in Stinson Beach. There were no Freedom of Information Act supports for the existence of the program, and no quotes about it, but it makes for an interesting proposition. The structure is still there, but the new owners remodeled it. Now it is just a private home in a beautiful location.

3. Waterfront

T he Waterfront Crime District covers the path of San Francisco's border with the sea. San Francisco started as a great port to provide access to the interior of California. Ships docked to offload supplies and goods and to onload materials such as furs and precious metals. The waterfront also provided a gateway for a massive influx of people seeking their fortunes. The Gold Rush brought in so many fortune seekers on their one-way trips that the harbor filled with derelict ships, abandoned for lack of crews to take them home. The original waterfront, or Embarcadero, looked very different. The city filled in the cove in stages, moving the waterline to its current position building long docks to reach the deep water for ships to dock in the different tides. The city once had over 40 working docks and piers, stretching from the Ballpark in the South of Market District to Fisherman's Wharf on the north side.

The crimes of the Waterfront include many of the standard crimes, but also includes a few predators of note including multiple killers, a serial killer, and murderers on the run.

The Waterfront follows the waterline starting from the Bay Bridge to finishing at the Golden Gate Bridge. The Waterfront covers the Embarcadero and parts of several other districts. It goes into Fort Mason which was started by the Spanish in the late 1700's as a battery to protect the Bay. It is now a small decommissioned fort on the north end of the city, west of the Fisherman's Wharf. Marina Green is a large open space of grass north of Fort Mason. The city built Marina Green after the 1906 Earthquake with fill from the destroyed buildings. It is a transit scene and there are no crime scenes in it. The Presidio is a neighborhood now because after the government demilitarized the post, it became another part of the city. It guarded the Bay for over two centuries and did not escape having its own set of crimes. The Presidio is one of the most beautiful Army posts in the country, and one of the most visited. The Golden Gate Bridge requires a trip through the Presidio and is at the northwest corner of the Peninsula and Presidio.

The Waterfront Crime Scene Tour starts near the Cable Car turnaround at California St. and Market St. It ends at the Golden Gate Bridge.

3.1 Pier 14

Embarcadero near Mission, South of the Ferry Building
Crimes: Homicide and Robbery
Scene Status: Still there

On July 1, 2015 a San Francisco area woman Kathryn Steinle walked along the Embarcadero with her father and a friend. They were near Pier 14. Jose Garcia Zarate was nearby and found a wrapped gun under a bench. When he handled it, the weapon fired a single shot killing the woman.

The following day of July 2, 2015 before 6:00 AM a local news crew set up at the pier to do a piece on a shooting in the location. The reporter and cameraman were ready to go when a car pulled up to the curb and a man climbed out. He pistol whipped the cameraman and robbed him of his equipment. The robber also took the equipment of a second news crew.

The case wound its way through the courts. Garcia Zarate was found not guilty of murder, only a felon in possession of a handgun.

The shooter had several prior felony convictions and had been deported at least five times. The issue became a 2016 Presidential Election issue about Sanctuary Cities.

3.2 Ferry Building

Embarcadero near Market St.
Crime: Bombing, Terror, Social Cause
Scene Status: The Ferry building remains, although it has been remodeled to be a farmer's market

A Social Movement, a landmark, and tenant converged to make a crime scene. The SF Ferry Building has a long history as being a part of the city. Today people visit, browse, and spend money on expensive food at the Farmer's Market. Prior to the ubiquity of cars, and the bridges connecting the city to the east bay, the Ferry Building was a major transportation hub, for people and goods coming into the city. It cut several hours off the long way around through the south bay. The Golden Gate and Bay Bridges reduced the Ferry Building's importance. The California Department of Corrections office rented office space.

In 1971 the area was in social upheaval. A riot in San Quentin resulted in the shooting death of celebrity prisoner and activist George Jackson. He wrote, *Soledad Brother.* On August 27, 1971 at a bomb went off in the Ferry Building which housed the California Department of Corrections. No one was hurt. An alleged member of the Weather Underground, an offshoot of the Students for a Democratic Society, called authorities and gave what amounted to a press release explaining the reason behind the bombing, tying it to the revolutionary goals of the organization. No one was ever convicted for the crime.

Now the building houses a farmer's market filled with gourmet food and crafts.

3.3 Ferry Boat Murder

The *El Capitan* ferry, from Oakland to San Francisco
Crime: Murder
Scene Status: The ferries still run across the Bay

Laura D. Fair was an actress by trade, but her hobby was a string of failed relationships. She was married several times, and at least one of her marriages ended in the man committing suicide. The other relationships were short. In October of 1870, Mrs. Fair completed her latest divorce.

Alexander Crittendon was one of the city's elite attorneys, and had been in practice two decades. Several years before the murder, he met Laura Fair and they started a relationship. On November 3, 1870 Crittendon was escorting his family back from Oakland to San Francisco on the ferry *El Capitan*. A woman wearing a veil approached the family after they were seated. She pulled a pistol and shot Crittendon in the chest. He died two days later.

Fair was detained soon after the shooting with the pistol. Her defense claimed she was insane from the pain he put her through in their seven year relationship.

The case made its way through the court system and while she was convicted and set to be hanged on July 28, 1871, she was granted a stay. A court later acquitted her by reason of emotional insanity, and she was free to reenter society. After putting the trial behind her, Mrs. Fair chose to be a book agent. She died in 1919 at 81 years old.

3.4 Pier 7

Embarcadero near Broadway, North of the Ferry Building.
Crimes: Homicide
Scene Status: Still there

October 19, 2005 seemed like any other day along the waterfront in San Francisco. The pier was filled with sightseers and all sorts of visitors. One young woman was visiting Pier 7 with her three young children, and nobody in the area had any idea what would happen.

Lashaun Harris stripped her three children naked and threw them into the Bay. It was an ebb tide, meaning the water level dropped as it rushed out to sea as fast as six miles per hour. Authorities recovered only one of the children near Fort Mason.

Police arrested Harris at the scene. The courts tried and convicted her of second degree murder. Her defense claimed she was hearing voices, one of which was God telling her to do what she did. She was later declared insane.

3.5 Meiggs Wharf

Between Piers 39 and 45, Embarcadero and Powell Streets
Crimes: Fraud, Corruption
Scene Status: gone

North Beach as we know it has no beach, but it started like one. In the early days of San Francisco North Beach was a vast unsettled area north of downtown. When the city entered into the Gold Rush days, sand dunes stretched from Broadway to today's Fisherman's wharf.

Henry Meiggs was an entrepreneur from back east who came to California with lumber in 1849, which he sold for 20 times what he paid for it. He realized sawmills would make him very rich and set about to capturing his dream of making it necessary and easy for San Franciscans to buy his land and wood.

In 1853 Meiggs built a large L shaped wharf at Francisco Street, which was then the waterline. Today the area is occupied by Fisherman's Wharf, Piers 39 and 45. His business plan counted on the dock raising the value of property around it. Meiggs had a great reputation, and was referred to as Honest Henry Meiggs in a lot of circles, so when he started using City of San Francisco warrants to pay for materials people were more than happy to accommodate him. Those warrants were loans with interest to the consumer for goods or services; an early version of a credit card. Meiggs rang up an $800,000 debt with the help of his brother who worked for the city.

Meiggs' bills amounted to over $30,000 a month in interest alone. He decided to leave town on October 6, 1854. The fraud came to light after he left for South America with his brother and family. In South America he built railroads, and had his third act as a business man, dying there in 1877. He paid off all his fraud debts, and made efforts to return to San Francisco, but never did.

Ralston stopped his pardon, the guy who engineered the gold coin swap to make sure his bank did not founder. (See 1.4, and 3.6) In 1977 a judge quashed the indictment against Meiggs on the grounds Meiggs had rehabilitated himself.

3.6 Neptune Club

The Bay, The Neptune Club off the end of Larkin St.
Crime: Death
Scene Status: The Club is now known as the Aquatic Park

William Ralston is credited as the man who built San Francisco. He had a talent for business and cornered the market in servicing the silver mines. The Bonanza Kings were beholden to him, and his Bank of California since they controlled much of the action.

Ralston had other financial interests besides banking, including supplying water to San Francisco, and building the Palace Hotel. Of course, all of those projects require money, and when his main silver mine started to reduce its production, cascading problems started. Ralston found himself in massive debt.

On August 26, 1875 the Bank of California had a run on deposits. He had no coins to give to the depositors, unlike the time he engineered a solution from the Sub-Treasury. The bank had to shut its doors. Ralston resigned, and signed over man of his assets to his business partner, William Sharon. The assets included his estate at Belmont, and the Palace Hotel.

Ralston then went for an afternoon swim in Bay off the Neptune Club at the foot of Larkin St. His body was found later in the day, and he was declared dead of a stroke.

3.7 Fort Mason Hostel

Fort Mason Hostel, Fort Mason
Crime: Fugitive Hideout from homicides
Scene Status: Same Buildings

In December of 2001 the world was in upheaval, and San Francisco along with the rest of the US was still reeling from 9/11. Christian Longo's wife and three young kids were murdered in Oregon. Longo left the area, and made his way to San Francisco where he hid out. For a few days around Christmas 2001 Longo hung out at the Fort Mason Hostel, and ate dinner in the kitchen there. He applied to work at a coffee shop on Union St.

Longo did not stay in the city, and left the country. Authorities caught up with Longo in Mexico while impersonating journalist Michael Finkel. He was extradited back to Oregon and convicted of murder with a death penalty.

Finkel is a journalist who created a source for an article bringing trouble to his career. The real Finkel and the fake Finkel (Longo) later connected and Finkel wrote a book about himself and his conversations with his imposter.

3.8 Alcatraz Island Prison

San Francisco Bay, towards the Golden Gate Bridge
Crime: Fugitives, Social Cause
Scene Status: The Island is still there, with modifications for tourism, and damage

Alcatraz Island has had a long and colorful history. It started as a fortress guarding the bay. The US federal government turned it into a federal prison for its worst offenders in 1934. It has the obvious resemblance to other island prisons in history. The prison could hold 800 prisoners, occupying 12 acres of land on the island, 1.25 miles from land. The Rock had many famous residents: Al Capone, Birdman Stroud (who had a rep as mean dude) George Machine Gun Kelly, and Morton Sobell (atomic spy connected with the Rosenbergs).

On June 11, 1962 three inmates staged a bold escape. Frank Lee Morris, Clarence Anglin, and his brother John Anglin were bank robbers serving long sentences on, "The Rock." They created paper mâché heads to delay the discovery of their departure. They used a rubber raft to swim to Angel Island. Authorities recovered part their escape equipment but found no bodies. These would be elderly men today if they survived, and it is possible. Their wanted posters are available on the internet.

By the 1960's Alcatraz was winding down. Federal prisons were reducing, and Alcatraz was expensive to operate, and the federal government shut it down.

Alcatraz Island already had a colorful history with crime as most of the residents were criminal practices. As the prison faded in memory, a new force took over the island; the *Indians Of All Tribes*.

Starting in 1969 and continuing to 1971 several dozen protesters occupied the island and claimed it as theirs.

They even offered to buy the land from the US for $24, a figure made famous in the sale of Manhattan Island.

Richard Oakes was the leader of the Occupation Movement. When his 13 year old daughter fell and died, he and his family left. (Oakes was later shot in 1972 by a YMCA camp leader in a separate incident.) Public sentiment initially empathized with the occupiers, with several celebrities lending their faces and money to the cause. A fire in the warden's house and other destructive measures did not help the cause. When a boat of sightseers was shot by an arrow, public mood shifted. The protests wound down, and both sides compromised.

The prison remains are still there, and can be visited by a tour.

3.9 Angel Island

San Francisco Bay
Crime: Dueling and death
Scene Status: The Island is still there, with modifications for tourism

Angel Island today is a romantic getaway for people to get out of the crowded city. It was a part of a constellation of fortresses guarding the bay in its early days. The US government used it an immigration center, and it was a major point of entry form people coming to America, including prisoners of war.

Angel Island's most interesting criminal history is its setting as a dueling grounds in Gold Rush San Francisco. It was a wild time, and duels, although illegal, were common ways to settle disagreements. Duels at high noon on the main streets tended to get disrupted, denying the involved parties their chance at satisfaction. Duels were illegal in Gold Rush San Francisco, but they had strong appeal for settling disagreements, and Angel Island's remoteness appealed to duelers wishing to engage without interference.

On the night of August 19, 1858 William I. Ferguson and George P. Johnston argued in a San Francisco saloon. One is they were debating slavery and its issues. Another more plausible reason was over a girl. Rumor blames the argument over Johnston's girlfriend – a more probable cause by statistics and anecdote. The two agreed to shoot it out. Ferguson was an attorney, and member of the Know Nothing Party, and later the Democratic Party. He was author of anti-dueling legislation. Johnson was a Democratic politician, and served as sheriff back east before coming to San Francisco. Angel Island still retains historical structures along with picnic places, and trails.

On August 21, 1858 dueled on Angel Island. After four rounds, Johnson struck Ferguson in the leg. A doctor recommended immediate amputation for the shattered thigh, but Ferguson refused . By the time a physician amputated his leg it was too late, and he died.

3.10 Crissy Field

Mason St. and Crissy Field Ave., near the west end of Crissy Field
Crimes: Kidnapping, Prefame, and Sex
Scene Status: The overall scene is still there with modifications and removal of buildings

David Carpenter has a long history documented by the California's justice system. Six decades ago, he was at the beginning of his career. On July 12, 1960 Carpenter picked up his female coworker and after driving her around, Carpenter attacked her at a bunker near a road leading to a battery site at the west end of Crissy Field. He tried to tie her up with a clothesline, and attacked her with a hammer.

Carpenter was stopped by an MP in the area. When the MP intervened, Carpenter fired a pen gun in his face, but missed. MP Jewell Wayne Hicks shot him. Carpenter was later tried and found guilty of the assault. He was paroled in 1970 and would go on to a gory criminal career as a serial killer. He would become known in 1981 as the *Sleeping Lady Killer* who had done much killing in the shadows of Mt. Tamalpais. He also was called the *Trailside Killer*. He also has a violent criminal history in Santa Cruz County in Henry Coe State Park.

3.11 Presidio Jail

Building 1213 on Ralston Ave. west of Storey Ave.
Crimes: Social Change and Civil Rights
Scene Status: The overall scene is still there

The history of the Presidio began on September 17, 1776 when Spain controlled the area. They wanted to keep control and built fortresses in the area, including the Presidio. In 1821 Mexico declared independence from Spain and controlled the fort until the US took it over in 1848. The war in the Pacific in WWII was run out of the fort, and it was a departure point for plenty who served in America's western front.

During the Viet Nam Era, not everyone wanted to leave America to go fight. Like every military base, the Presidio had its share of prisoners. Its jail was building 1213, known as a stockade. The jail grew overcrowded, and prisoners were unhappy about the conditions. In 1968 the army still held prisoner work details on the post where they were attended to by guards with shotguns. In October of 1968 a guard shot an escaping prisoner. The prisoners grew more agitated, and Captain advised them to behave.

On October 14, 1968 27 prisoners took part in a, "mutiny." Many civilians might call it a grievance session by prisoners. They were formed up for the morning assembly and the 27 out of over a hundred prisoners sat down, chanted and sang songs. They asked to see a Captain, within a soldier's rights. One prisoner read their demands. They had several, including an end to work details, but the most interesting was a demand was for the staff to receive psychological evaluations.

Several of the protestors were arrested for Uniform Code of Military Justice Article 94, which is intent to usurp or override a lawful order. They received sentences of varying lengths. On appeal all sentence were reduced to no more than a year.

The Presidio remained a key base until the end of the Cold War. In 1989 the fort became slated for closure but preserved in the process. Building 1213 is still there with the number on the walls, and bars on the windows.

3.12 The Golden Gate Bridge

North end of the San Francisco Peninsula connecting to Marin

Crime: Deaths

Scene Status: The Bridge still stands

The Golden Gate Bridge is alleged to be the bridge with the highest number of suicides in the world. About every two weeks, one person jumps off the bridge. The unofficial total is now over 1500 deaths, making the Golden Gate Bridge one of the most investigated crime scenes in San Francisco, and anywhere else in the world.

Most deaths at the bridge come from suicides of jumpers. A few people fall off by accident during protests. People have lived the fall, and there are a few who have made the fast trip down twice. Bodies reach an estimated 75 to 80 miles per hour before crashing into the water below making it more like a freeway crash than a jump into water.

An interesting bureaucratic issue is who recovers the body. People who land on the outside of the Bay fall into the Coast Guard's jurisdiction. People who land on the north half of the Bay are under Marin County's jurisdiction. Those who land on the south half are in San Francisco County's jurisdiction. Those who are not recovered may not get counted. Considering all the suicides over the decades of the bridge, it is possible not all jumpers were voluntary.

Citizen groups have advocated to build a barricade to prevent such jumpers. They should be completed in the 2020's at a cost of over $200,000,000. The entire bridge cost $35,000,000 to build in the 1930's.

Popular culture keeps the Bridge in center view. Most crime movies set in San Francisco include the bridge such as *The Presidio, Vertigo, Dark Passage, Planet of the Apes*, and a *View To A Kill* with James Bond.

4. Central

T he Central Crime District covers the lands of San Francisco's early westward expansion. The district includes three different neighborhoods: Union Square, Nob Hill, and the Tenderloin.

Union Square got its name from the Union after the North won the Civil War. Union Square became the uptown center boasting all sorts of ways to spend money and live the good life. The area is filled with high end boutiques and shopping catering to those with a taste for expensive things.

Nob Hill is a granite outcrop of high elevation where the city's elites have made their homes for as long as the city has been around. Famous Nob Hill residents include Leland Stanford and his family, along with his other three partners who built the Transcontinental Railroad: Charles Crocker, Mark Hopkins, and Collis Huntington. All four of them, and many more newly wealthy had opulent palaces on the hill. The Great Earthquake of 1906 damaged many homes there. The fires caused by the quake did as much or more damage. Many mansions met their ends through the zealous application of dynamite as a means of stopping the fire.

The Tenderloin's origins remain in the fog of time, but there is speculation it took its name from a New York City neighborhood, or from police graft which provided enough bribery for patrol officers to eat the best cuts of steak. Another legend refers to prostitutes, and parts of their anatomy. Tenderloin is a village within the city offering a counter to the sleek images elsewhere and an island where the non-conventional people fit in. Many of the dens of sin moved in after the 1906 Earthquake. But the Tenderloin is more than just a rough place to visit. It is a neighborhood of tolerance. While Union Square provides a model for things to buy to fit into the pinnacle of society, the Tenderloin provides a model for people being who they are, especially if it does not fit into society.

The crimes of the Central District have shocking elements and shows how crime can be anywhere. Union Square has a row of boutique shops that used to house inhumane brothels, and a hotel party scene resulting in death. Nob Hill is home to wealthy homes and luxury hotels. The Tenderloin is the center of art theft crimes, homicides, and hideouts.

The Central District is bordered to the north by California Ave. and to the east by Grant Ave. It is bordered to the south by Turk St. and to the west by Larkin St.

The Central District Crime Scene Tour starts at the Cable Car turnaround at Powell St. and Market St. It ends at Bush St. and Taylor St.

4.1 Flood Building

870 Market Street at Powell
Crime: Celebrity, Corruption, Fraud, and Murder
Scene Status: Similar, remodeled

The Flood Building is an office building named after James C. Flood, who rose to fabulous wealth in step with the city. Flood started as a bartender, and gathered enough information to build a mining fortune and diversify to keep it. The building on Market at Powell was completed in 1904, and survived the earthquake, making it a central location for the rebuilding of the city. It was the preeminent building, and anyone who was anyone had an office there.

Dr. Nathan Houseman was one such person of prominence in the city in the 1920's and '30's. His reputation as a physician was a bit shady, and he was later sent to prison in 1941 for perjury.

In 1921 San Francisco elected attorney Frank Egan its first Public Defender. Egan surrounded himself with a cast of characters. His process server Albert Tinnin had been convicted of manslaughter but was still hired for the Public Defender's Office.

In April 1932 Mrs. Jessie Scott Hughes was an elderly woman who lived across town and had nothing to do with Dr. Houseman. Police had wired Dr. Houseman's office in the Flood Building to listen to his conversations. By chance, the authorities learned of Mr. Egan's plans to take the elderly woman's money, and maybe even kill her. Supposedly, attempts were made to warn her, but Mrs. Hughes would have none of it. She was found the victim of a hit and run accident. Upon a close look, authorities found the accident had been staged, and she was held down by thug while another ran her over with a car. The case revealed money as the motive when Egan was both Ms. Hughes' lawyer and her beneficiary. The San Francisco District Attorney tried Egan for the murder and he was found guilty and sentenced to 25 years in prison.

Another tenant of the building was the local office of the Pinkerton Detective Agency. Pinkerton was a civilian spymaster in the Civil War, and then for industry. One of his operatives in the San Francisco office was Dashiell Hammet, who must have picked up interesting story lines investigating various mysteries in San Francisco.

4.2 Tait's Café and Radio Show

24 Ellis St. north of Market St.
Crime: Celebrity, Obscenity, Social Cause, Precrime
Scene Status: Now a parking structure with a café in the same location

Ray (Rae) Bourbon was a drag queen who broadcast a radio show from the café every evening at 10 PM. Bourbon was quite famous in the world of cross dressing performers and also performed with Mae West during other shows. He was arrested during the middle of the broadcast in 1933. Criminalizing drag queens seems unthinkable today, but it was a real issue back in the day. The show, "Boys Will Be Girls," all fit into the, *Panzy Craze*. The *Panzy Craze* was a period in the late 1920's and early 1930's where open gay culture was popular. The establishment responded by targeting of members of the Craze with so-called decency and obscenity laws.

In the 1950's Bourbon claimed to be the first to receive gender reassignment surgery in the Western Hemisphere.

Decades later, Bourbon made an appearance in the criminal justice system when was unable to pay for his pets' stay in a kennel. The owner sold Bourbon's pets for medical research. Bourbon became obsessed with the issue, to the point of writing the governor about it. In 1968 the elderly Bourbon was convicted of murdering the dog kennel owner along with two others. He was given a long sentence and passed in a Texas prison.

4.3 Maiden Lane

Maiden Lane Alley, between Union Square and Grant
Crime: Prostitution
Scene Status: The alley has been renamed and reformed

The Barbary Coast had a long run, and it roots go back to before the City of San Francisco even started. Back in the day, Maiden Lane was called Morton Street, and was an area rampant with prostitution. When the 1906 Earthquake struck it was renamed Maiden Lane as part of the marketing for a new image. Authorities moved the prostitution off. Today the Lane is filled with bridal shops and boutiques. The street is a pedestrian mall during the day with the ends secured by gates.

140 Maiden Lane is the only Frank Lloyd Wright building in San Francisco. He completed it in 1949.

4.4 Hotel St. Francis

12th floor, 335 Powell St. at Geary St.
Crime: Death, Attempted Assassination of President
Scene Status: Same building with renovations

The St. Francis Hotel was and is a great hotel in a city of great hotels, and it has over a century of greatness looking out over Union Square. On Labor Day weekend 1921 in suites 1219. 1220, and 1221, Roscoe "Fatty" Arbuckle and movie star friends were having a party in the hotel.

The star held a party in the hotel and it is reputed to include all the elements a celebrity party should, alcohol, sex, drugs, rock and roll (for the 1920's). When young starlet Virginia Rappe took ill, she took a break from partying, but did not leave the suites. Medical treatment came later. She was hospitalized and pronounced dead. An autopsy named her cause of death peritonitis, an infection brought on by a hole in a person's intestines causing an infection in the abdomen.

Ms. Rappe's demise had a lot of people weighing in and sold a lot of newspapers. Arbuckle was accused of raping and murdering Ms. Rappe. He stood accused in three sensational trials. The court acquitted Arbuckle, but the media stories had ruined him. Arbuckle did behind the scenes work with a pseudonym, but never regained fame and fortune like he had before. He died at the young age of 46 in 1933.

The *Jazz Singer* Al Jolson died of a heart attack in room 1219 during a poker game in `1950. He was famous for being one of the biggest movie stars of the 1920's and starred in the first talking movie.

Over half a century after the Fatty Arbuckle scandal, on September 22, 1975 President Gerald Ford was in San Francisco at the hotel. Squeaky Fromme had attacked him in Sacramento 17 days earlier, so his security detail had to be on high alert for any sort of assassin. The President was out front of the hotel preparing to leave.

Sara Jane Moore stood on the other side of the street and fired a .38 pistol. Oliver Sipple was a Marine Corps veteran wounded in action in Vietnam and taxi driver. He was a hero in the crowd who thwarted the plan and prevented her from killing the President or anyone else.

According to a US Secret Service, "Public Report of the White House Security Review," Moore was employed with the *People In Need* group, which was funded by Hearst as a result of his daughter

Patricia Hearst's request as a part of the SLA. She was also an FBI informant, and had been arrested the day before with a concealed handgun.

Sipple's life changed and he became famous. He was already an active member of the gay liberation movement and worked with Harvey Milk, but he was also closeted from his family back east. He requested the media leave his personal life out of the story, but he was too good a hero. Sipple's heroism put him in the public eye. The papers outed him, which ostracized him from his family. He sued the media, but the courts ruled his personal life was public news. He died in 1988.

4.5 Crocker Mansion

Corner of Cushman St. and Sacramento St.
Crime: Celebrity and Nuisance
Scene Status: New buildings

Sometimes crime takes on comic tones for everyone except the people in the crime. Nicholas Yung was a prosperous mortuary operator in the city. Yung had arrived to the US in 1848 and built his home on top of Nob Hill because land was available and he liked the location. The city grew and Nob Hill progressed into a desirable place to live.

Enter Charles Crocker. In the 1860's he one of the wealthiest men in San Francisco and America after his role as one of the Big Four who built and controlled the Transcontinental Railroad. The man could have almost anything he wanted. By 1876 he bought up all the houses he could on the block of California St. and Cushman St. to build his mansion. All houses except the one holdout Yung.

Yung had the misfortune to build his home before Crocker on the northeast corner of Cushman St. and Sacramento St. Crocker wanted to build his mansion on the entire block as was befitting a man of his stature. The two haggled over the price of the land without coming to a resolution.

Crocker decided to build a wall around his neighbor. He built a 40 foot wooden fence to block out the sun, putting Yung's home in perpetual shade, blighting his garden. This continued through 1880 with Yung's death. His widow moved out, but kept the property. Crocker died in 1888, still unsuccessful in his quest for the whole block. By 1895 the property was more of a storage lot, with a fence around it. The city refused to take action about the fence since it was legal. Yung's widow died in 1904, and her daughters sold the land to Crocker's heirs in 1905. The 1906 earthquake came and destroyed the mansion, the cottage, and everything else on the block. Crocker's family donated the land to the Grace Cathedral.

Spite fences continue, but this was an early version and there were no laws about it. In 1956 the State of California enacted laws limiting fences to six feet.

4.6 Hotel Mark Twain

Room 203, 345 Taylor St. at O'Farrell St.
Crimes: Celebrity and Drugs
Scene Status: The overall scene is still there, with modifications, and new ownership

Billie Holiday is recognized today as a jazz great with the postage stamp to prove it. On January 22, 1949 she was riding high, and in town for performances. Then police found an opium cigarette in her room. She was arrested. Her trial ended with her being found not guilty. Today, her career, and status as a great, are untarnished.

4.7 The Bristol Hotel

56 Mason St. at Eddy St.
Crimes: Murder and hideout before they were famous
Scene Status: The overall scene is still there, with modifications

The Bristol Hotel in the Tenderloin is a residential hotel close to Market Street. It touts itself as being in Union square, but it appears to be more like the Tenderloin. In fact, the plaque out front lists it as being on the National Register of History Places, courtesy of the Uptown Tenderloin Historic District. It was built in 1908, and has been called the Athens Lodgings and the Hotel Belmont.

The *Night Stalker*, Richard Ramirez is associated with Los Angeles. In 1985 he was captured in East LA by a mob of angry citizens. The LAPD saved him from being killed by them when they showed up. Before that Ramirez stayed in room 315 of the Bristol in 1984-5. He was the main suspect in the slaying of Peter Pan of August 17 1985. The victim's wife identified him. He was later linked to the Tenderloin killing of 9 year old Mei Leung in the basement of 765 O'Farrell from April 10, 1984. All told he was convicted of 13 counts of murder, 5 attempted murders, 11 sexual assaults, and 14 burglaries. Ramirez died on Death Row in 2013 while awaiting execution.

Bristol Hotel resident and radical feminist Valerie Solanas died in room 202 on April 25, 1988. Ms. Solanas was a part of Andy Warhol's New York scene in the sixties at *The Factory*. She also self-published her work, *The SCUM Manifesto*. A publisher offered her a deal, but she grew wary of him, and decided he and Andy Warhol were conspiring against her. On June 3, 1968 She attacked Andy Warhol by shooting him, hitting him one of three shots. She also shot Warhol's colleague who considered publishing her. She received a three year sentence, along with psychiatric care. After jail, and follow up stalking of the artist, she moved west. She found her second act at the Bristol Hotel, where she would later die of pneumonia.

4.8 Compton's Cafeteria

101 Taylor St. at Turk St.
Crimes: Civil Rights, Obscenity, and Social Cause
Scene Status: Building torn down

Compton's Cafeteria is no longer there, but it serves as a landmark for the people involved in the battle for equality for transgendered persons. The cafeteria was open late night, and as the neighborhood hosted many colorful people in the city, the cafeteria hosted its share of them.

Transgendered persons have faced challenges finding acceptance, even in a city such as San Francisco. Although there are examples of drag queens with spectacular success as entertainers, the majority are ostracized and subjected to obscenity laws.

The Tenderloin had a thriving community of all sorts of people. The '60's was still a time when people were arrested for cross dressing. Compton's Cafeteria at 101 Taylor became a hangout for a lot of the trans community late night. Of course, when people hang out at businesses and spend money there are few complaints by the business. However, events can spiral out of control.

August 1966 was a tough time at the cafeteria. A particular drag queen was no longer welcome in the restaurant, and when police went to arrest her, all hell broke loose. The riot erupted, and there were broken windows, and unrest. The Stonewall Riots of 1969 get all the press in New York, but the San Francisco Tenderloin Riots predates them for being the start of the Gay Pride Movement three years earlier. There is even a documentary about the riot called, *Screaming Queens: The Riot at Compton's Cafeteria.*

4.9 Cambridge Hotel

Room 601, 473 Ellis St. at Leavenworth St.
Crimes: Art
Scene Status: Intact

San Francisco has a lot of art around in both museums and galleries. The Cambridge Hotel in the Tenderloin is a residential hotel built in 1926 and used as a residential resource for homeless.

Terry Helbling is one of the residents in the Hotel and lived in room 601. There are articles on Helbling describing him as a savant, but he seems to be a person who liked to look at nice art. He turned his 10 by 10 studio into a gallery, and furnished it with stolen artwork from local galleries. He took paintings by artists such as Alexander Baxter and Jean Mannheim as well as many other prints from the Botanical Library.

The law caught up to the art collector and returned the purloined pieces to their owners. The courts also restrained him from visiting various galleries, and museums throughout the city.

4.10 Weinstein Gallery

383 Geary St. at Mason St.
Crime: Art Theft
Scene Status: Intact

Picasso is a sought after artist in San Francisco as the rest of the world. July 5, 2011 started like a lot of other days in the Tenderloin when the Weinstein Art gallery opened. They were showing Picasso's sketch, *Tete de Femme*, valued at $275,000. It was drawn in 1965, and belonged to the artist's driver.

A thief from back east entered the store, took the painting, and jumped into a waiting taxicab to flee. Simple plan, less to go wrong. Until the heist unraveled with the help of Lefty O'Doul's Bar. They provided video footage of the thief and he was apprehended not long afterward. The painting was recovered. The thief was later convicted.

4.11 Pinecrest Restaurant

401 Geary Street at Mason
Crimes: Murder
Scene Status: The overall scene is still there, with modifications

The Pinecrest Restaurant is modeled as a classic American diner. The booths, the flooring, the food, all conjure a traditional way of eating. One where the customer is always right, and the people working there had worked there for a long time. Restaurant manager Helen Menicou and cook Hashem Zayed knew each other well as they spent over two decades together in the diner.

Twenty years is a plenty of time to have arguments and on July 2, 1997 Ms. Menicou had reportedly corrected Zayed in front of customers for making a customer poached eggs which was off the menu.

The following day July 3, 1997 the two came to work as always. Zayed produced a pistol and shot Ms. Menicou in front of customers and killed her. Zayed was found guilty of murder and died a few years later in prison of a brain tumor.

4.12 Dennis Sullivan Fire Chief's House

870 Bush St. near Taylor St.
Crime: Vandalism and Arson
Scene Status: Private facility

San Francisco is like a lot of mature cities with buildings from times past repurposed. The Fire Service has many buildings around town employed in new ways. The Dennis Sullivan Fire Chief's House is a beautiful building at 870 Bush St. In 2008 the city allowed the its Planning Director John Rahaim to reside at the building while house hunting.

All was well until the employee got into a fight with his boyfriend. Lance Farber vandalized the home and lit the bed on fire. He fled the scene, and was arrested in another county. He was charged with arson and causing $50,000 damage to the historic building. He later settled with the city for under $20,000. He also earned the moniker of the fire-starting, tomato tossing man.

Two years later Lance Farber died in his sleep at 49 years old. He was a chiropractor by trade whose license was in jeopardy due to unprofessional conduct and his troubles with the law.

5. Lower Interior

The Lower Interior Crime District mostly in the neighborhood south of Market. South of Market or SOMA feels very different than north of Market because the two grids meet at Market and are diagonal to each other making for interesting navigation through the town. San Francisco's City Planner Jasper O'Farrell made Market St. 120 feet wide in the 1850's knowing the town would grow up around it. The street has been the main artery in town ever since.

SOMA grew from small businesses and residents into a warehouse district. The railroad terminates in SOMA making it ideal for light industry. Now the area has mostly white collar businesses along with housing. Many bars and restaurants to accommodate the residents. The railyard is still there, mostly servicing commuter traffic. The baseball stadium started holding games in 2000.

The Lower District also includes the Civic Center neighborhood which is north of Market, about one and three quarters mile from the Ferry building. The Civic Center Neighborhood is the seat of power in the city. San Francisco moved City Hall and many of the administrative offices west from the area of Chinatown, and the Financial District to a few miles after the 1906 Earthquake.

The crimes of the Lower Interior District come with all the intrigue one would expect from government centers including many crimes of violence and murder, along with terror, intrigue, espionage, and corruption.

The Lower Interior District has its east border at the Embarcadero. Its south border is about half a mile south of Market

St. The district's west border is the Central Freeway Offramp. The district crosses Market St. with an east border of Jones St. Its north border is Turk St., and its west border is Van Ness Blvd.

The Lower Interior Crime Scene Tour begins at the Cable Car turnaround at the intersection of California Ave. and Market St. The tour ends at Polk St. and Turk St.

5.1 Rincon Hill

Bay Bridge Anchorage
Crime: Social Change and Death
Scene Status: The area has been rebuilt from warehouses to offices and residences

In the 1930's San Francisco had many warehouses south of Market catering to industries in the area. It was also a time of upheaval with the Depression serving as a background. With all the hard economic times there was bound to be a fight over money. The fight in San Francisco came in the form of labor versus the captains of industry. Depending on who you identify with, labor was fighting for their rights, or bleeding the industry dry.

The controversy erupted into violence on Bloody Thursday, July 5, 1934. It took place near the Embarcadero and from Market street to Rincon Hill, on up to Second Street. The fight had 1000 police against 5000 marine strikers and their sympathizers. Later 2000 guardsmen were dispatched to the waterfront.

There were shootings as well as tear gassing. A major part of the fight was along Steuart St. from Market to Howard. Police hurled tear gas bombs into the headquarters and wounded were dragged inside. Two men were reported as killed.

The strike and riots got bad enough to cause a stoppage of all work on the San Francisco-Oakland Bay Bridge. Workers had to be called off the job on the anchorage and mainland piers because they were in the battle zone.

5.2 Southern Pacific Building

65 Market St. at Steuart St.
Crime: Bombing, Terror, Murder, and Social Cause
Scene Status: building remodeled and rebuilt, bomb damage still visible

San Francisco was like a lot of America during World War I. The people had access to enough news about the meat grinder was less than enthusiastic about getting into it. By Summer 1916 it was clear America was not going to be isolationist for much longer. The German Navy had threatened American trade and shipping. Not everyone agreed it was a good idea. Anti-war and isolationist feelings were common with radical organizations as International Workers of the World and among mainstream labor leaders.

Business organized a Preparedness Day Parade. Planners worked on a massive parade set to last three and half hours, with over 50,000 marchers, over 50 bands and 2100 organizations like military, civic, judicial, state and municipal divisions as well as newspaper, telephone, telegraph and streetcar unions.

On July 22, 1916 The Preparedness Day parade started around 1:30 and a little after 2:00 a suitcase bomb exploded on the east side of the Southern Pacific Building, at 65 Market St. It was on the west side of Steuart Street, south of Market Street. The explosion killed ten people and wounded 40.

Two radical labor leaders, Thomas Mooney and Warren K. Billings, were arrested and tried for the attack. The trial was alleged to have been plagued with false witnesses and biased jury foremen. The two men were convicted, despite widespread belief they had been framed by the prosecution. Mooney was sentenced to death. Two weeks before Mooney's scheduled execution, Stephens commuted his sentence to life imprisonment, giving him the same punishment Billings. President Woodrow Wilson along with several other leaders pressed the California Governor to examine the case. In 1939 the case had fallen apart, and new Governor Culbert Olson pardoned both men based on evidence of perjury and false testimony.

No other person was convicted as the Preparedness Day bomber.

5.3 South Park

3 South Park, off of 3rd St. and Brannan St.
Crime: Art, Murder, Prefame and Celebrity
Scene Status: The planned neighborhood is still there, with modifications

Eadweard Muybridge was an artist from England who was an early adopter in the field of photography. Muybridge also had the artist name Helios for an early part of his career. His 1860's and 70's photographs of the American West are among the earliest in existence. In fact, he photographed Yosemite long before the more famous Ansell Adams.

Art and creativity do not always mean an easy life. Muybridge had personal problems. The home at 3 South Park is the most preserved San Francisco home of the artist, and is a place he lived before he killed his wife's lover. Muybridge career as a photographic great is marked by a killing in the middle of it.

The artist Muybridge married a pretty young wife, and settled down to start a family. Of course, an older male who is often away and involved in his work may not be able to attend to his wife's needs. Muybridge and his wife had a child, and suspicion centered on a young man with whom the wife was friendly.

Drama critic Major Harry Larkyns was the man who was cheating with Muybridge's wife. Tired of being cuckolded, Muybridge travelled to Calistoga to kill his wife's lover on October 17, 1874. He did not flee the scene and was taken into custody. A not guilty by insanity plea was denied, but the trial acquitted him on the grounds of justifiable homicide.

Muybridge went on with his life. In 1878 Muybridge became the brains behind the first moving picture showing a running horse, but a few things had to come together to make it all work. At the time, Leland Stanford was already a hyper wealthy railroad tycoon who sponsored the artist. Stanford and his colleagues had a bet to determine whether all four of a horse's hooves left the ground during running. Muybridge set up a series of cameras with tripwires to trigger the pictures as the horse ran by. Muybridge put the films in sequence, and the outcome of the experiment is movies. Plus, he proved all four of the horse's hooves do leave the ground. Muybridge is credited with the 24 frames per second standard.

5.4 Palace Hotel

2 New Montgomery St. at Market
Crime: Death and Espionage
Scene Status: Rebuilt in 1909 after the 1906 Earthquake

The Palace Hotel has a past tied to its creator, William Ralston. Ralston made a lot of money from mining, and then lost a lot of money in the Great Diamond Hoax of 1872. Depending on how a person sees Ralston, either he was building way more hotel than little San Francisco needed at the time as part of a plan to help the city arrive to major metropolis status or he had ownership of a bunch of land south of Market Street and he wanted to develop it and profit. The hotel was opulent at a time when many San Franciscans lived in tents.

The hotel opened in 1875 as a showcase for modern living. At the time Ralston's finances were in disarray. Within the year he resigned as bank head, and died the same day, leaving the hotel and the rest of his assets in the hands of William Sharon. (See 3.6)

The original building was destroyed by fire after the 1906 earthquake. The current building was built in 1909. Earthquakes and fires aside, the Palace survived to become a scene for many crimes and other events.

An early famous death at the hotel was King Kalahaua on January 20, 1891. At the time he was King of Hawaii and visiting San Francisco. The Spreckels family ran a sugar company, and lived in San Francisco, so it would be logical for the King to come visit the city.

In 1903 Lillie Coit got into a scrape in the Palace Hotel. An employee shot another former employee while trying to protect Lillie.

One of the most interesting parts of crime history at the Palace was its involvement as a residence for foreign powers. Wilhelm von Brinken was the German Consulate during WWI. He operated the San Francisco cell of the terrorist operation out of his residence at the hotel. The Hindu German Conspiracy involved him, and his office. (See 5.10)

In 1923 the Palace hosted the death of President Warren G Harding. The death controversy seeds were sown started long before the final breath. President Harding's administration was plagued by scandal including the Teapot Dome, and more domestic scandals such as those involving mistresses and illegitimate kids. There is no evidence for a murder, but the President's death includes two big motives, love and money. The Presidential yacht shipped south from Alaska as part of his reputation rebuilding tour. By the time the ship put into San Francisco, the big man was ill. The stated cause was food a lot of other people ate, and had no problem with. In any event, the president lingered for a bit and passed in suite overlooking Market Street on August 2, 1923. The case has always been a medical death from illness. There was no autopsy.

Nikita Khrushchev made a speech in the dining room during his historic visit in 1959, which may make it a crime scene.

The Palace Hotel Bar on the ground floor is a great place, even today. Famed reporter Herb Caen said Kalloch (of feud with DeYoung fame, see 5.7) won the mayoral race in 1879, and as a Baptist minister he ran the city from the old building of the Palace Hotel Bar. The new building has a wonderful on the wall behind the bar, Maxfield Parrish's painting of the *Pied Piper*.

5.5 Marriot Marquis Hotel

780 Mission St. at 4th St.

Crime: Burglary and Celebrity

Scene Status: The building is still there

Alex Trebek has long been a famous game show host with a legion of adoring fans. In July of 2011 he was in town for a competition and on the 26th he went to bed, preparing for more appearances the following day. He must have been very surprised to wake up on the 27th to a woman rummaging through his luggage. Trebek took matters into his own hands and chased down the thief. In the process he tore his Achilles tendon.

5.6 4th and Howard

Intersection of 4th St. and Howard St.

Crimes: Assault

Scene Status: Everything has changed, other than the streets

Fire Companies have a great history of saving people, and places, but they have not always been municipal departments. The first fire companies in the US were volunteer outfits promoted by Ben Franklin. Soon there were volunteer fire companies everywhere, along with for-profit ventures. The for-profits would charge an annual subscription for protecting buildings. In cases where no firm had a contract to protect a building competing fire companies would arrive and fight over who got to fight the fire, and collect a fee.

New York had a huge influence on San Francisco of the 1800's. Fire companies in New York were also a political force. Many of the political bosses employed the firemen as people to, "encourage," voting (in the right way, of course). Many of the earliest key players (tough guys) in San Francisco came from New York; David Broderick, Charles Duane, Cora.

On December 17, 1885 Howard Co. #3, Knickerbocker Co. #5, and Monument Co. #6 met up and had some kind of disagreement. Whether it was politics, or money, has been lost in time. By the end of it, Edward Flaherty was shot in the arm.

5.7 The Old Mint

88 5th St. near Mission
Crime: Assault and Celebrity
Scene Status: The steps remain

Isaac Smith Kalloch was a minister who had a reputation as a ladies' man, which was hardly new, and frontier people tended to be more forgiving for indiscretions. Kalloch was the minister of the Baptist Metropolitan Temple church. It was located on Bartlett near 21st Street, in what is the Mission district, but was torn down around 1915. Kalloch had political ambitions and decided to run for mayor on the Workingmen's Party ticket. His party was founded by disaffected whites who organized around an anti-Chinese platform. Kalloch had been through an adultery trial in Massachusetts.

Charles DeYoung, along with his brother Michael, owned and published the *Chronicle* newspaper. In 1879 during the run up to the election the two sparred. *The Chronicle* became embroiled in the mayoral run and was critical of Kalloch. It published lurid details about the candidate. He also accused the candidate of being tainted and going after votes in bars.

Kalloch fought fire with fire, and promoted his own stories of the de Young's family history. He made up a story about how DeYoung was the child of a whore, raised in an environment of ill repute.

Charles De Young shot Isaac M. Kalloch in his leg in front of the Old Mint, at 88 Fifth St. in the summer of 1879. The minister recovered and became a one term mayor. The newspaper publisher stayed in jail over night for the crime, and paid a fine. DeYoung would not live to have a trial for attempted murder (see 1.17).

5.8 End Up Bar

401 Sixth St. at Harrison St.
Crime: Attempted Murder, Death, and Fraud
Scene Status: The bar remains similar with minor updates

The San Francisco bar scene can be brutal as any war. The End Up bar on Sixth Street has a long and colorful history as being a gay party bar among party bars, but all are welcome to come dance and enjoy the culture. Al Hanken opened it in 1973, and along the way built a loyal clientele for events like its wet jockstrap dance contest on Sundays, and its Fag Fridays. It also catered to the transvestite crowd.

The bar cruised along, and went through a family of owner and managers. Three Hanken brothers owned the club. The middle brother Helmut Hanken inherited the club from his brother in 1989 and died in 1993. Helmut also hired attorney Douglass Whitmore to manage the business. The club started having financial problems under Whitmore, such as not paying taxes, labor disputes, and being in Chapter 11. When Helmut died in 1996, he named Whitmore as his executor to the business, and his estate. Carl Hanken took the normal legal steps any smart business owner would do, and used the courts to wrest control from Whitmore. The courts agreed Whitmore had mismanaged the business.

On July 24, 1996 Carl Hanken was at home in the suburbs with his wife when Whitmore showed up in a disguise and shot him. The suspect was on the run for a week and a half and shot himself after being cornered by police. He died of his own wounds, but the bar has survived and continues to thrive.

5.9 Colossus Disco

Nightclub 1015 Folsom, Folsom and 6th St.
Crime: Celebrity, Precrime, Serial Killer
Scene Status: Club is still there, different name

Andrew Cunanan was a man who was going places, according to what he was saying about himself. In the 1980's he grew up in a nice part of San Diego, and came North to San Francisco to find his dream. Cunanan acted as a male escort, and overall man about town. There is no mention of him having any marketable skills for gainful employment.

Cunanan reinvented himself, moving to the city. He also developed his aliases, one of which was Navy Lieutenant Drew Cummings.

In October of 1990, Richard Strauss's opera, *Capriccio* opened at the San Francisco Opera House across the street from City Hall. Gianni Versace designed the costumes. As with all VIP's, Versace was invited to take in the local nightlife. He went to the Colossus Disco, 1015 Folsom St. In the VIP room Versace met Andrew Cunanan for the first time. There is no record of how Cunanan was a VIP other than being around VIP's.

Cunanan has no history of any San Francisco crimes, but in April and May 1997 Cunanan killed four people as he made his way across country to Florida. The first two were men he shared history with. The third and fourth victims are reported to be strangers, and may have been convenient targets in the pursuit of means to get to the primary target. On July 15, 1997 he killed Gianni Versace outside his Miami home as he returned from a store. Then Cunanan killed himself on a nearby houseboat.

5.10 Federal Courthouse

The James R. Browning Federal Courthouse 95 7th St. and Mission
Crime: Espionage and Murder
Scene Status: The building remains, although modified

The Federal Courthouse in San Francisco is the kind of place one would expect crimes to be reconciled. The building was damaged in both the 1906 and 1989 earthquakes, but has been restored. In 1971 it was listed on the National Register of Historic Places, and houses the Ninth Circuit Court of Appeals.

In WWI, the US was under attack by terror cells supported by Germany. The majority of the attacks were on the east coast, in places like New York, and Washington, but San Francisco was in on the action too.

In 1918 the courthouse became a crime scene the most expensive trial in its day. It took place in the US District Court in San Francisco and lasted from November 20, 1917 to April 24, 1918. A number of Indian nationalists were accused of conspiring with the Germans during World War I.

The plot involved shipping guns to India for the purpose of aiding a rebellion. The rebellion would have drawn resources from Great Britain to deal with it. The plot was also called the Annie Larson Plot, after the ship to be used in smuggling the arms. German money bought American arms to ship to India. The accused had violated US neutrality and attempted to cause a rebellion in India. Since Germany was at war with Great Britain, Germany would have an advantage when Great Britain had the distraction of a rebellion. At the time, America claimed neutrality. The affair took on the title of *The Hindu-German Conspiracy Trial* and encompassed members of the Ghadar Party, as well as members of the German consulate in San Francisco. The German spies operated out of the Palace Hotel (See 5.4). Ram Chandra was the chief conspirator.

The trial wound down when on April 23, 1918 Ram Singh shot Ram Chandra in the courtroom. Then US Marshal J. B. Holohan shot Ram Singh. US attorney Preston witnessed the shootings.

The 9th District Court of Appeals occupies the building today. Other trials held there include those of Napster, Affirmative Action, Same Sex Marriage, Tokyo Rose, Union leader Harry Bridges.

5.11 Black Self Help Moving and Storage

1645 Market Street at 12th St.

Crimes: Hideout, Mass Murder, Social Cause, Terror
Scene Status: Building still there, most else has changed

In the fall of 1973 and spring of 1974, San Francisco was plagued by a series of shootings. They appeared random in the beginning, but were tied to a radical sect of anti-white and anti-establishment black Muslims who called themselves the Death Angels. The Death Angels were an offshoot of the Nation of Islam. There were fourteen fatal attacks, and eight more injuries from the shootings all over the city, but the densest concentration of attacks was the area around the Civic Center. A .32 caliber pistol tied the shootings together.

The investigation centered on Black Self Help Moving and Storage on Market and 12th. San Francisco Homicide Inspector Rotea Gilford was one of the detectives working the case. According to investigative accounts, including the book *Zebra*, by Earl Sanders, the business employed men who were of a radical sect of Islam. When they were not moving or storing, they sought to avenge the wrongs perpetrated against black people by white people. The warehouse was a place to meet and plan their acts. The investigators also named it a place where torture took place. The case went to trial in 1975 and had 108 witnesses. Four men received life in prison for their roles. The business is gone, but the low buildings along Market Street west of Van Ness are still there.

5.12 Mechanics' Pavilion

99 Grove St. at Polk St.
Crime: Celebrity, and Corruption
Scene Status: Rebuilt after the 1906 Quake, now the Bill
Graham Civic Auditorium

Wyatt Earp still ranks as the embodiment of the American Tough Guy. He is characterized as a law enforcement officer unafraid to step outside the law to do what was right. Children relive his shoot out at the OK Corral in playgrounds across the country.

Wyatt Earp's fight at the OK Corral was in 1881 in Tombstone Arizona. He gained fame and notoriety from it, but he also left Arizona. In late 1882, Wyatt Earp, and his brother Warren left Colorado and joined Virgil Earp in San Francisco. Wyatt reconnected with his love interest Sadie, AKA Josephine Marcus and stayed with her for the next 47 years.

On December 2, 1896, Wyatt Earp refereed the Fitzsimmons vs. Sharkey Heavyweight Championship fight at the Mechanics' Pavilion. The location of the Mechanics' Pavilion is the present day Bill Graham Civic Auditorium, near city hall, the library, the State Building, and Asian Art Museum. Wyatt Earp had refereed over 30 boxing matches before the Heavyweight Championship Match in question.

The fight itself was illegal under San Francisco law, but was well attended by government officials including police officers. Women fought for and won the right to attend the fight, as they had been forbidden to attend such events in the past.

The match started under a bad sign when Police Captain Whitman arrested Earp for carrying a concealed weapon and confiscated the pistol from him at the boxing match. The following day an arrest warrant was issued for Earp. He was taken into custody and released on $10 bail. On December 4, 1896 he paid a $50 fine to make it right.

Fitzsimmons was favored by as much as 3:1 going into the fight. The fight came down to a referee's decision. Earp awarded the fight to Tom Sharkey, due to Bob Fitzsimmons hitting him when he was down. Most of the crowd seemed to believe Fitzsimmons won the fight. Fitzsimons and his party protested, and there were lawsuits back and forth. A judge heard the case and ruled since it was an illegal fight, he had no jurisdiction. Earp's decision stood.

5.13 City Hall

1 Dr. Carlton B Goodlett Place , Polk St and McAllister St.
Crimes: Celebrity, Corruption and Murder
Scene Status: The overall scene is still there

San Francisco City Hall is a grand building with a grand history. It sits on the west end of the Civic Plaza, and has been featured in the news many times. The old City Hall near Portsmouth Square was the poster child for corruption. It took 27 years to build and millions of dollars in overruns to build the new facility which was completed in 1899. Insult to injury to the taxpayers, the 1906 earthquake razed it in 90 seconds. The public demanded to hold a person accountable, and powerbroker Abe Ruef was the guy. The building of City Hall was a metaphor for all the corruption plaguing San Francisco's government from utilities to prostitution. (See 2.8). The new, new City Hall was completed in 1915. The City Hall can be identified by its dome and columns. City Hall continues to be a crime scene.

In 1978 Supervisor Dan White had resigned his position on the San Francisco Board of Supervisors. He then changed his mind and wanted back on. He appealed to the Mayor without success. On November 27, 1978 White snuck into City Hall by an open window to avoid the metal detectors at the doors. He murdered Mayor George Moscone, and Supervisor Harvey Milk in their chambers by with his .38 caliber pistol. Milk was the first openly gay elected official in the state of California. The case went to trial and the world learned of the Twinkie Defense, which purported a junk food diet could lead to depression and bad decisions. White was found guilty of manslaughter, and given a sentence of under eight years. Members of the public rioted in front of the building, showing their displeasure with the ruling.

White was released after five years in prison and committed suicide in 1985.

5.14 Federal Building

450 Golden Gate Ave. at Larkin Ave.
Crime: Corruption, Drugs, and Fraud
Scene Status: Same

Crime places are changing. With cyberspace, the locations of crime takes on new meaning since it happens across several locations: the suspect's location, or the victim's, a third location, or in between on the transmission. The Federal Building houses many offices including the FBI.

The *Silk Road Investigation* was a huge undertaking looking into a black market on the internet. The Silk Road catered to the drug market most, but it had an anything goes ethos. Everything was available for a price, and the transactions were conducted in anonymity. People paid for the goods with digital currency, making for a multilayered challenge.

The FBI investigated the case, along with the assistance of other federal law enforcement agencies. They did a great job figuring out the case, and arrested a man who they considered the mastermind - Dread Pirate Roberts, the online persona for Ross Ulbricht. The took him into custody at the Glen Park branch of the San Francisco Public Library. The courts found him guilty and sentenced him to life without parole. Of course, along the way, the investigation for the government evolved into a personal investigation, and a few agents decided crime does pay.

According to news articles, in March of 2015 the FBI arrested two former agents who worked on the Baltimore Silk Road Task Force. The two agents worked their own angles on the investigation and studied the suspect. After the authorities arrested Dread Pirate Roberts for being the brains behind the Silk Road Dark Web site, the two rogue agent took over and got in on the wire fraud, money laundering, and stealing digital currency. Then they became the objects of an investigation.

5.15 California Hall

625 Polk St. at Turk St.
Crimes: Obscenity
Scene Status: The overall scene is still there, with modifications

San Francisco's Castro District gets all the press as the center of gravity for the gay community, but on December 31, 1964, there was a New Year's Eve Party at California Hall at the corner of Polk and Turk. At the time, gay events tended to be open secrets rather than open events. The building was built in 1912 with funds from the German community who were planning on using it as a community center. It was also used to film scenes in *Dirty Harry*.

The organization holding the costume party event was the Council on Religion and the Homosexual, (CRH) which was a group of religious leaders and gay community leaders who combined to work together. Over 600 attendees came to ring in the New Year. They were photographed, and publicized. The police wanted in, and lawyers for the group denied them entry, which resulted in their arrest. The ACLU defended them, and everyone was acquitted after. The gay community was provided with an SFPD liaison and San Francisco shifted away from prosecuting so-called morality laws.

6. Upper Interior

he Upper Interior Crime District covers a crescent route through the center of San Francisco. It is a large geographical area in residential districts. As San Francisco expanded its footprint, it grew west to create more neighborhoods for residents including Polk St. or Polk Gulch, Cow Hollow, Pacific Heights, and the Fillmore.

Parts of the Polk Gulch neighborhood look similar to the Tenderloin, and it has also into a place for good food and entertainment. Cow Hollow is south of Marina Green, and is so named because it was once a farm. Pacific Heights overlooks Cow Hollow and the Bay. It is a traditional bastion of wealth and power overlooking the Bay and the Golden Gate Bridge. The Fillmore is south of Pacific Heights, and west of Polk Gulch. The neighborhood which has been subject to several upheavals over the years with massive movements of different cultures including Jews, Japanese, and African Americans.

The Upper Interior is mostly residential neighborhoods built around business streets. The neighborhoods give little clue to the types of crimes hosted in them. The area has suffered from a high number of bombings, along with a number of grisly murders, and a fatal dog mauling.

The Upper Interior District's north border is Bay St. and its east border is Larkin St. Its south border is Golden Gate Ave. and its west border is Lyon St.

The Upper Interior Crime Scene Tour begins at the intersection of Olive Ave. and Van Ness Ave, south of Geary Ave. The tour ends a few miles west at Geary Blvd. and Fillmore Ave.

6.1 British Motors

901 Van Ness Ave. at Olive St.
Crime: Celebrity, and Theft of an Automobile
Scene Status: Same

British Motors has beautiful cars and it is one of the great luxury car dealers in the city. In 2011 celebrity chef Guy Fieri's yellow Lamborghini was in the service department for some work. The vehicle screams celebrity: flashy, high performance, expensive, and unique.

A thief stole the ride and security video captured his action that looked more Hollywood than San Francisco. When he fled with the car, the thief left a rappelling harness at the scene.

There was no conviction in who stole the car. The car ended up in the possession of a Max Wade in his storage locker. The story in the newspapers indicates the youth wanted to use it to impress a woman he was interested in dating.

6.2 Mitchell Brothers' Theater

895 O'Farrell Street, at Polk St.
Crimes: Celebrity and Obscenity
Scene Status: The overall scene is still there with modifications

The Mitchell Brothers O'Farrell Theatre was founded by Jim and Artie Mitchell in 1969. They created an adult entertainment venue as well as a production facility to produce many popular films at 895 O'Farrell Street. They produced and directed many adult films, including *Behind the Green Door* in 1972. The movie cost $60,000 to produce and grossed over $25 million, making it a profitable venture. One of their final movies was *The Grafenberg Spot* (1985), featuring the underaged Traci Lords, who had entered the adult-video industry with fraudulent identification.

Late journalist Hunter S. Thompson was a close friend of the brothers, and spent time at the O'Farrell Theatre. He cast himself as manager of the establishment.

In 1991 Jim killed Artie in suburbia, not at the theater. The trial featured the first animated virtual reality reenactment of the crime in California. It was cutting edge and precedent setting. Several dignitaries turned out in support of the accused, including former Chief of Police turned Mayor Frank Jordan, as well as a former Sheriff. Jim then served three years of a six-year voluntary manslaughter sentence.

A light hearted crime story about the location takes place in the early 1980's. The Mayor of San Francisco was Diane Feinstein. She wanted to take a tour of the theater, and one of the owners advised her to buy a ticket. Afterward the marquee of the theater advertised show times could be obtained by calling a phone number. The phone number was the mayor's unlisted personal number.

6.3 Great American Music Hall

859 O'Farrell St. at Polk St.
Crimes: Art and Prostitution
Scene Status: The overall scene is still there with modifications

The Hall was built in 1907, just a year after the Earthquake destroyed much of the town. It was part of the new wave of brothels which spread out in the city since attention focused on rebuilding the Barbary Coast as a wholesome zone. The Hall has a main room with private areas on the sides. The decorations are like an opera house.

The Great American Music Hall may have started as an ornate brothel but it changed to its second act of musical entertainment. Now hip and cool bands play there. It is a small venue built to hold 600 people and is in a colorful part of the Tenderloin. It is on the same block as the Mitchell Brothers' O'Farrell Theater.

6.4 Geary St. and Sutter Ave.

Intersection of Geary St. and Sutter Ave.
Crime: Bomb, Social Cause, and Terror
Scene Status: Repaved streets

The iconic San Francisco Cable Cars have not always been a city run public transportation service devoted to a few scenic tourist lines. They started as a private invention by Andrew Hallidie in the early 1870's based on mining equipment. In the 1880's San Francisco had many street car companies. Even Governor Leland Stanford owned one. Wages were low and workers struck toward the end of 1886.

On December 28, 1886 a worker was inspecting the lines on Sutter St. at the intersection with Van Ness Ave. He removed a cover from a malfunctioning wheel, and located several explosives. His reaction was to transport the bombs to police headquarters where they were declared bombs.

The strike dragged on into 1887. There had been several other cable car bombings in the city, including Post St. between Larkin St. and Polk St. also at the intersection of Sutter St. at Dupont St. (Now Grant).

By February 1887 the police had a suspect the bomb placed on the lines at Sutter St. and Van Ness Ave. On February 16, 1887 at 4:30 AM police followed J. E. Stiles after he left his home at 412 Larkin. They ordered him to stop, and when he ignored their orders, they shot at him ten times. All shots missed, and the fracas turned into a foot chase. Stiles threw an item over a fence, which police recovered and found to be a bomb. Stiles explanation was he was trying to gather evidence against another man, and he had no intention of bombing anything.

After police arrested Stiles, they went to the home of his friend and co-conspirator H. C. Dean. Police searched his home and found dynamite. Dean's excuses rivaled Stiles for unbelievability when he said he had no idea how the explosives got in his house. As it happened, both men were carmen on strike from their jobs at a cable car company.

6.5 Royal Theater

1529 Polk St. near Sacramento St.
Crime: Bomb and Terror
Scene Status: New Buildings, the façade remains

San Francisco has had more than its share of bombings. The bombers have had political, religious, or social messages. The Royal Theater on Polk St. had its own bombing relating to a labor issue.

The Royal started out about a decade after the 1906 Earthquake and was later one of s string of theaters owned by the Nasser family. The Castro Theater was another in the group. Architecture enthusiasts will appreciate it was designed by James and Watson Reid who also did the Hotel Coronado in San Diego. It was later remodeled by Timothy Pflueger to give it the Art Deco style visible today.

On June 1, 1930 an explosion damaged the projection room. Stories vary from dynamite to pipe bombs being the cause of it. At the time the theater was modernizing, and transitioning from live musicians to recorded sound. The musicians were out of jobs. The other workers in the theater, such as projectionists, supported them, and also struck. Nonunion labor was called in. Then the explosion. The case was never solved.

In one of the recent housing crunches a developer tore down the theater to build apartments, but kept the façade.

6.6 Alhambra Theater

2330 Polk St. near Green St.
Crime: Bomb and Terror
Scene Status: Building repurposed, the façade remains

San Francisco movie theaters had a difficult transition from live musicians to a recorded sound. The Alhambra Theater is down the street from the Royal. It was a grand old theater, decorated in the Moorish Revival style reminiscent of the Middle East, and Spain. Minarets complete the look.

After the Royal Theater on Polk St. had its bombing all was peaceful for about half a year. On October 18, 1930 employees located a dynamite bomb at the ticket booth. No one was hurt, but police estimated it could have razed the block.

The theater has been repurposed as a gym. The façade remains, and it is easy to imagine the theater as it was.

6.7 Laguna and Greenwich

Car parked at the corner of Laguna St. and Greenwich St.
Crimes: Murder and Organized Crime
Scene Status: The overall scene is still there with modifications

San Francisco does not have the reputation as a Mafia town compared to many other cities, but it has had its brushes. In the late 1930's as America was emerging from its Prohibition debacle, Nick DeJohn was building his career in the Chicago Mafia. At the time Al Capone was in Alcatraz. A series of reorganizations left several of his friends dead, and him with impression that it was time to leave.

DeJohn changed his address to Santa Rosa, his name to Rossi, and developed the image of a furniture dealer He got involved with the San Francisco Outfit and all was well for a decade.

On May 5, 1947 police found his body in the trunk of his own car parked at Laguna and Greenwich. He was killed by garrote.

6.8 The Bus Stop Bar

1901 Union St. at Laguna St.
Crime: Corruption
Scene Status: Same

On November 20, 2002 two men were in the Bus Stop bar and restaurant getting fajitas to go. Three males came up to them and demanded their food, and their request was denied. A fight broke out with the two people getting injured and the three men leaving. They were stopped, and released.

Bar fights without arrests are common. Police often dust off the involved players and admonish them to behave. Everyone avoid a court case and a potential record. In this case the fracas involved three off duty San Francisco Police officers. The two civilians who claimed they were assaulted alleged a cover up. The issue had numerous court cases, and the men were acquitted of all criminal charges. There was a civil judgment against one officer, and a lot of movement around positions in city government. The press dubbed the event *Fajitagate*.

6.9 Hindu Temple

Hindu Temple, 2963 Webster at Filbert St.
Crime: Bombing, Murder
Scene Status: Still there, remodeled

San Francisco and the Bay Area had an immigrant population from India who brought the Hindu faith with them. The Hindu

Temple at 2963 Webster St. was credited as being the first Hindu Temple in the Western Hemisphere. Swami Trigunatita designed and built the temple when the congregation grew. The structure includes elements of traditional Hindu architecture blended with local style. It was dedicated on January 7, 1906. It survived the Earthquake a few months later.

On December 23, 1914 local convert Louis Vavra showed up to services in the temple. He was a machine shop technician. He grew frustrated at his slowness to understand what the texts meant. Vavra exploded a bomb in the temple and died from the blast at the scene. Swami Trigunatita lingered for a few weeks, and succumbed to his injuries.

The temple continues to operate as the Vedanta Society and welcomes visitors. Their website provides information about various lectures open to the public.

6.10 Six Gallery

3119 Fillmore St. at Filbert St.
Crime: Art, Civil Rights, and Obscenity
Scene Status: Building is still there, different occupants

The Six Gallery was like a lot of small galleries in San Francisco of the 1950's. It was another outpost for the growing arts scene emerging on the West Coast. The Six Gallery was formed in 1954 by five men and a woman; 5 + 1 = 6. They took over from the previous King Ubu Gallery in the same location.

In the 1940's Alan Ginsberg was put out of the Army and settled in San Francisco. He used his creative talents for business during the day, and writing at night. He lived in North Beach and worked in the Financial District.

On October 7, 1955 the Six gallery held a poetry reading with several poets. At the time, its significance was not known, but when Ginsberg read *Howl* read at the Six Gallery on it would go on to be credited as the first event of the Beat Generation. *Howl* became known as the opening shot of a literary and philosophical movement that included Kerouac's *On the Road*.

Herb Caen of the *Chronicle* called the people *Beatniks* on April 2, 1958, although the concept of the Beat Generation had been around for a while. By 1957 *Howl* had been published and the owner of City Lights Bookstore, and publisher Lawrence Ferlinghetti along with his manager Shigoyeshi Murao ended up in a court battle over the book . (See 2.10)

6.11 Russian Consulate

2790 Green St. at Baker St.
Crime: Espionage
Scene Status: Building still there, not a consulate anymore

On August 31, 2017 the US State Department ordered the Russian Consulate in San Francisco closed within two days, and as of September 2, 2017, the facility remains closed. The diplomatic snub was the result of allegation of Russian meddling in America's 2016 election. But the Russian Consulate has a long history of activity, and like all consulates it has a cloud of suspicion relating to espionage hanging over it.

The US and Soviet Russia have had a tense relationship with each other since start of the Cold War after WWII. The end of Cold

War has done little to bring the two nations closer. The consulate's location in a residential neighborhood seems odd, until looking at a map. The consulate is right outside the Presidio which was a major nerve center for the US military on the west coast. The consulate was a few hundred feet from a major military installation, but miles away from downtown where many other nations had their consulates.

6.12 Washington and Cherry

Washington St. and Cherry St.
Crime: Murder and Serial Killer
Scene Status: The streets remain

The Zodiac Murders are a famous series in the San Francisco Bay Area. The Zodiac, or an imposter claiming to be him, was active in press in the late 1960's to early 1970's around San Francisco. He is credited with a body count of four men and three women. Publicity seems to be part of the killer's style. Someone claiming to be him wrote letters to the press, and published ciphers, giving the murders a game aura.

On October 11, 1969 an unidentified man got into a cab at Mason and Geary in the Tenderloin. His destination was Washington and Maple in Presidio Heights, but the driver, Paul Stine had him stop at Washington and Cherry, a block west of the original destination.

The suspect shot the victim in the head with a 9mm pistol and took a piece of bloody shirt as a souvenir, as well as the victim's wallet and keys. The bloodstained shirt scrap was later mailed to the newspaper. DNA might help solve the crime today, but a cab has a lot of DNA floating around it, so it would not be easy.

San Francisco's first African American homicide detective, Inspector Rotea Gilford, worked on the case. Melvin Belli (see 1.7) agreed to go on a radio broadcast for a call in opportunity for the murderer, but it went nowhere in terms of solving the crime.

6.13 Julius Franklin House

2930 California Street, between Broderick and Baker
Crime: Murder
Scene Status: New Buildings

Frank Miller was a butler in the home at 2930 California St. His employer was Mr. Julius L. Franklin. On February 14, 1896 at around 5:00 AM gunfire was heard in the basement, and Miller lay unconscious on the floor with a flesh wound to his neck. An intruder lay dying nearby with a bullet hole in his head. The intruder was Billy Murray, an out of work man.

Miller said he acted to protect the home and lives of the people there. No evidence countered his statement. His employer was loyal to the butler, and supported him. Detective Lees looked into the case, and found several problems with it.

First, Miller's coincidental history caused an alarm. A year prior on the same day Miller thwarted a burglar in the basement at 3:00 AM and fired off his pistol doing so. The burglar fled after assaulting Miller. Miller was rewarded by his employer and persuaded to stay, despite his voiced concerns about the suspects returning to even the score.

Second, CPT Lees learned the butler met the burglar Murray before the crime, near Portsmouth Square by the Barbary Coast. He convinced him to come back to his house, and Murray being without money agreed.

Police convinced Franklin of his employee's potential involvement in murder instead of protection, but Miller never was prosecuted for the killing. Miller relocated to Santa Barbara where he assaulted a young girl within a short time, and by the end of 1896 was in prison on a five year sentence.

6.14 Alta Plaza Apartments

11th floor, 2500 Steiner St. at Jackson St.
Crime: Homicide
Scene Status: Still there, Secure building

The building at 2500 Steiner stands out because it is a tall building on a tall hill. The building was built in 1926 and has 12 stories, versus the two or three storied mansions around it. The building is an old style apartment tower. It looks like the kind of place where wealthy, private, responsible people live.

Two residents were attorneys caring for the pair of killer dogs in a nice apartment. Some of their lawsuits focused on conditions in prisons. Marjorie Knoller and her husband Robert Noel lived on the 11th floor. The two cared for dogs belonged to a man who was incarcerated. These were two large Perro de Presa Canario dogs trained as guard dogs.

January 26, 2001, Diane Whipple returned from shopping. She paused in the hallway of the 11th floor outside her apartment. Marjorie Knoller was returning from a rooftop visit with her dogs Bane and Hera. One of the dogs escaped her control and mauled

Ms. Whipple. The second dog joined in. Ms. Whipple died of her injuries.

In court both Noel and Knoller were found guilty of manslaughter. Ms. Knoller was also found guilty of second degree murder. She appealed the charge, and it was upheld in 2016. As of 2020 she remains in prison. Noel died in 2018 after spending less than a year in prison. Ms. Whipple left behind her domestic partner Susan Smith who sued the lawyers for wrongful death. One of the prosecutors was Kimberly Guilfoyle who became a tv analyst.

6.15 Sally Stanford House

2324 Pacific Ave. between Webster and Fillmore
Crime: Burglary and Prostitution
Scene Status: New owners, Private residence, do not disturb

San Francisco's sex industry has been well established and documented. The people in the industry are also well established and documented. Many of San Francisco's prominent citizens have had pasts far worse crimes than selling sex, so when a madam's home is burgled, it is not news.

Sally Stanford is a true tale showing how San Francisco is the land of Second Acts. He real name was Mabel Janice Busby when she was born in Oregon in 1903. She was a madam in San Francisco after WWII, and catered to the United Nations crowd who were in town to decide how to run the world. In 1950 she expanded across the Bay to Sausalito. She became a successful restauranteur after opening Valhalla. She also morphed into a civic leader when she ran afoul of city ordinances about signage. The public elected her to the Sausalito City Council and then mayor in 1972.

On April 8, 1965 a San Francisco newspaper reported Sally Stanford was in the hospital recovering from a heart attack when a band of thieves including three felons and two dirty police officers were arrested for breaking into her home. Stanford had reported the event prior claiming a premonition, and the crooks were caught.

6.16 Fillmore Auditorium

1805 Geary Blvd. at Fillmore St.
Crime: Art, Celebrity, and Murder
Scene Status: The Auditorium still stands

The Fillmore Auditorium is sometimes called the birthplace of the 60's sound out of San Francisco. Janis Joplin, the Grateful Dead, and Jefferson Airplane all got their breaks there. Bill Graham is credited with helping them do so, as he ran the place.

The auditorium was built around 1912 and was called the Majestic at first. The focus was dancing. Time marched on, and the neighborhood changed. By the 1950's a new order was in the area, and the Fillmore District was the epicenter of Black Culture and Music in the city.

The Fillmore District has long been an area of upheaval. The neighborhood has seen waves of different population groups including Japanese, Jews, and African Americans. America's internment of Japanese during World War II left many vacancies in the community filled by African Americans who settled in the area. The 1960's were a period of upheaval for the neighborhood which was populated by African Americans. At the same time, there was a movement on to carve out a section of the Fillmore for Japan Town, and widen Geary into a major artery.

Charles Sullivan was an early driving force behind getting great Motown acts for the Fillmore which he had renamed from its previous moniker of the Majestic. He was a well-respected member of the African American community. He also had business dealings outside the group. Bill Graham was a man on the way up, and he and Charles Sullivan were able to cut a deal allowing Graham to start presenting shows in the Fillmore. The venue was no longer catering to one group, but serving multiple cutures.

Charles Sullivan, the man known as the Mayor of the Fillmore was found lying dead next to his car on August 2, 1966. There was a gun nearby. His place of death was Fifth and Bluxome Streets, which is down by the train station. It was an industrial part of town, where he had no recorded business interests. The case remains unsolved.

The auditorium was sold to the Nation of Islam for it to hold its services and became Nation of Islam Temple #26. In the 1970's several members of what would be the core group of Zebra Murders Death Angels were attending services there.

6.17 Jim Jones Temple

Geary, west of Fillmore, now a Post Office
Crimes: Celebrity, Mass Murder and Social Action
Scene Status: New Building

The Reverend Jim Jones was a celebrity church leader in 1970's San Francisco. He was a fiery preacher who started in Indiana, moved to rural California, and upped his game to San Francisco. He preached love and understanding. His flock grew. He called his organization *The Peoples Temple*, borrowing ideas from Marx and Lenin. He had a history as both a civil rights leader and a faith healer.

Being as well organized as he was, he was able to rub elbows with a lot of politicians, including Mayor Moscone, Willy Brown, Walter Mondale and anyone else who wanted a reliable block of voters. In February 1978 Harvey Milk even wrote a letter to President Carter supporting Jones.

The Temple operated out of the building where the Post Office now stands, and it was a meeting place for the Peoples Temple.

The temple was going along smoothly, with articles about it in the news, and a growing congregation. In the shadows there were complaints of family members of congregants who said they were unable to reach their loved ones. Allegations of financial oddities drew the government's interest. Jones and other leaders decided San Francisco was too intolerant and in 1973 set about to finding a new place. Within a few years they leased land in Guyana to build a socialist farm. By 1977 the Temple felt too much pressure in San Francisco, and moved hundreds of people to Jonestown, Guyana. Guyana can be a beautiful place, when not seen from the perspective of a starving missionary. The people made a go of it, and the leader's decisions seemed to be more and more irrational.

Meanwhile back in the US, enough people complained about the group to cause CA State Senator Ryan and his entourage to have a look. They flew down with a news crew. Accounts of their visit were like a Potemkin village presenting a choreographed show of a religious socialist utopia. The real situation was more severe. The visit set off a crisis and shootout occurred at the airport, with Temple members murdering the Senator, and wounding future State Senator Jackie Speier.

On November 18, 1978 over people 900 died from suicide encouraged by their reverend. Jones told his followers the Guyanese army would soon invade their compound and gave the order for followers to drink grape Flavor Aid laced with cyanide. Jones had been stockpiling cyanide for several years before the suicides. He also instructed them to poison their children first. The settlement's medical staff assisted with administration of the cyanide, and it worked in about five minutes. More than 300 of the dead were children. Only 33 people survived. Jones chose to shoot himself for his suicide.

The temple was torn down. A post office stands on the lot now.

7. Out West

T he Out West Crime District covers the Western Districts of San Francisco. These are some of the newest sections of town, although well over a century old. This tour covers the Haight, Golden Gate Park, Outer Sunset, and Lake Merced.

Haight Street started as a residential neighborhood near Golden Gate Park. Haight Ashbury's defining time was the late 1960's around the Summer of Love. Haight has a reputation for its hippie culture, sex, drugs, and rock'n roll. Many musicians including the Grateful Dead and Janis Joplin lived there. The drug culture had its own philosophical doctrine promoted by several people including Timothy Leary. The Haight also served as a base for some of the parties and events in nearby Golden Gate Park.

Golden Gate Park is one of America's great municipal parks. It starts near the heart of city and goes west for three miles until it reaches the Pacific Ocean. Golden Gate Park has been key part of city culture, especially as a gathering place. It started as an idea in the 1860's based on the other great parks in the US such as Central Park in New York city. At over a thousand acres, it has everything including museums, arboretums, a zoo, an aquarium, and plenty of open space. It also held Kezar Stadium, where the 49'ers used to play football. It goes three miles until it terminates at the Pacific Ocean.

The Richmond District is the area to the south of the Presidio. Developers started making it into suburban housing in the later nineteenth century. The 1906 Earthquake increased that need and eventually it filled up like the rest of the city.

The Outer Sunset neighborhood is part of what was once called the Outside Lands. In the early days of the city, the western area was called Outside Lands because it was outside the city limits and had yet to be tamed. Some early photographs show the area as an endless stretch of sand dunes. The area grew up, and became a housing tract for the residents who continued to pour into the city. Today most people call it the Sunset District.

The different zones within the Out West Crime Scene Tour offer a variety of crimes including terror, murder, and robbery, along with social causes.

The Out West Tour's east boundary is Divisadero Ave. The north boundary is the north edge of the Richmond District where it meets with the Presidio. The west boundary is the Pacific Ocean. The south boundary is Merced Lake.

The Out West Tour begins at its eastern edge at Buena Vista Park next to Haight St. The tour ends at Lake Merced near San Francisco State University.

7.1 Buena Vista Park

Near the tennis courts on the East side, Haight St. and Buena Vista Ave. East
Crime: Death, Arson, and Sex
Scene Status: The park is still there

Buena Vista Park has the distinction of being the oldest public park in San Francisco. Its neighbor park Golden Gate gets a lot of press for crime scenes, but tiny Buena Vista showed it could compete in 2011. The park is on Haight Street, and goes up a hill. The park also has a lot of recycled stone from graves moved out of the city when San Francisco passed an ordinance in 1900 banning burials inside city limits.

The park has also established itself as a place for people to go for a casual romantic interlude in the bushes. On June 10, 2011 police started investigating a dead man's burned body near the recycling bin near the tennis courts. Within two weeks police arrested a man who explained he knew the dead man from prior liaisons. The evening in question they met in the Castro and made their way to the park to have sex.

According to the Medical Examiner the death was caused by asphyxiation. The trial found the suspect responsible for the death of the man whom he had strangled as a component of consensual rough sex. The burning part came after the sex and death. According to the accounts of what came out in trial, the surviving half of the duo panicked and threw the dead man into a recycling dumpster and lit it on fire. The defense attorney proposed the idea his client was burning recycling in order to summon authorities for help. There was also a 911 call, and a pulled fire alarm.

The manslaughter and accompanying charges resulted in the convicted man being released for time served at the end of the trial. The same man made the news again in 2015 when he was arrested for an arson on the 4000 block of 18th Street, near Castro Street.

7.2 Nureyev Party House

42 Belvedere St. at Waller St.
Crime: Celebrity and Drugs
Scene Status: Private Residence, do not disturb

The Summer of Love was in full swing in the Haight. On July 11, 1967 police were called to a home for a wild party. While marijuana has been decriminalized, back then drugs were still against the law. As police went through the partygoers, they came across celebrated ballet dancer Rudolf Nureyev who admonished them it was not a party until he arrived. His dance partner Margot Fonteyn was also there. Police arrested the ballet dancers along with several others for marijuana possession and took them downtown to the jail.

When Nureyev was released from jail to a crowd of paparazzi. He called them children. The DA dropped the charges.

7.3 Manson House

636 Cole St. near Haight St.
Crime: Precrime
Scene Status: New residents, Private, do not disturb

The Manson family's crimes happened in the LA area, but before the murders he lived in Haight Ashbury, basking in the atmosphere of tolerance and drugs.

Charles Manson spent a lot of time in prison, and adapted well to it. He even warned a parole hearing it was not a good idea to release him. They decided otherwise, and in March of 1967 Manson was released from prison. He spent a little time in Berkeley and moved across the bay to the home at 636 Cole. He lived there in the Haight from April 1967 to July 1967. During that time, he picked up strays and runaways, integrating them into his, "family." He left for LA in an old school bus, and in August 1969 the Tate La Bianca murders happened.

The Summer of Love of 1967 crashed down with the Manson Family Murders in the minds of the American public. The revolutionary behavior of sex, drugs and rock and roll were seen as hedonistic self-indulgence shattered by a few people who used the situation to take advantage of others and kill them.

7.4 Haight Fire

1700 Haight St. at Cole St.
Crime: Arson, Social Cause, and Terror
Scene Status: A new unrelated building is on the site

In 1988 the Thrifty Drugs chain started to build a store in the Haight, at Haight and Cole. There were protests from individuals as well as from the neighborhood preservation group. A predawn fire at the under-construction building woke most everyone up in the neighborhood. Those still asleep woke to the 150 firefighters who came to put out the blaze in the five alarm fire; half the city's force on duty. Eight surrounding buildings were collateral damage, including a 60 unit apartment complex. The Haight Ashbury Free Clinic was also burned as a part of the fire.

The strongest indicator of arson was the two five gallon gasoline cans in the basement. Thrifty Drugs chose not to try it again, and shelved plans to open a store.

7.5 Witch Killer House

Basement apartment, 825 Shrader St. at Beulah St.
Crimes: Murder
Scene Status: Private Residence, do not disturb

On March 7, 1981 police responded to an apartment in the Haight at 825 Shrader. Karen Barnes had lived there with her two roommates, Michael and Suzan Carson. Someone bludgeoned her with a frying pan, and stabbed her. The killer left her lying in the kitchen. The other two were nowhere to be found. The apartment was described as having no modern things, such as a TV. It was without utilities, and decorated by odd drawings.

The Carsons were on the run for two years after the Barnes killing, but they helped themselves to be located when Michael Carson sent a letter to newspaper columnist Herb Caen from Sonoma County Jail complaining their crimes did not receive news coverage in a big city like San Francisco. They were in jail for a roadside murder in Santa Rosa. One of the Karen's friends saw the note in the newspaper, and notified the authorities. They investigated and arrested the couple for the murder of Karen.

A lot of the information about the crime was collected from the Carsons when they gave a several hours long jailhouse press conference to KGO Radio and the *Chronicle* newspaper on the killings. Michael Carson was willing to talk, but he stipulated he wanted a press conference to discuss his religious views. Prosecutors and police refer to it as a confession, while the couple might have called it news. The killers had a doctrine, and wrote their own manifesto for their beliefs, called *Cry For War*. They cited their reasons for killing Karen as being rooted in her false conversion to their faith, which they self-identified as vegetarian Moslem warriors. Their mission was to rid the world of witches.

The two talked about three different murders they committed and gave details on all of them. They later pled not guilty, and were convicted of Karen Barnes' murder, and two others. Their press conference provided many details about their actions.

7.6 Golden Gate Police Station

1899 Waller Street, west of Stanyan St.
Crime: Bomb, Murder, Social Cause, Terrorism
Scene Status: Still there, updated

The San Francisco Police have lost officers over the years for various reasons. Police are a common target for people's dissatisfaction with the government, and there is plenty of dissatisfaction in the city, most of which results in protests with signs.

The Park Police Station is one of the oldest stations in the city. While most other stations are in neighborhoods surrounded by other buildings, the Park Station is a stand-alone building in the park. The architecture reflects how it was built for horse drawn police vehicles, and there is a turn-around in front, and buggies did not have reverse. The compound has been modified to fit the times and it is now surrounded by a chain link fence, razor wire, and blocks on the windows. The public still has access to the walk-up window in the lobby.

On February 16, 1970 a suspect walked up to the lobby window and planted a pipe bomb filled with heavy staples. Sergeant Brian McDonnell was killed in the blast, and nine other officers were wounded. The case has never been solved and no one has been convicted of the crime. In the early 2000's the case was reopened as a cold case, and suspicion has been focused on a radical group dedicated to anti-imperialism and often associated with bombs, but as of 2020, no one has been held responsible.

7.7 DeYoung Museum

50 Hagiwara Tea Garden Dr. near John F. Kennedy Dr.
Crime: Art and Burglary
Scene Status: Museum rebuilt. Still there.

The M. H. DeYoung Memorial Museum in Golden Gate Park is a great museum with a great collection. Christmas Eve 1978 was almost like any other night. The difference being thieves used the skylight to enter the museum, and leave with the painting, *Portrait of a Rabbi* by Rembrandt, and two others.

Rembrandt Harmenszoon van Rijn, commonly referred to by his first name alone, was a Dutch painter who lived from 1606 to 1669. The DeYoung Museum was funded by the DeYoung family. (See 5.7 and 1.17) The family made their money from their newspaper, the *Chronicle*.

After the theft, the painting vanished from public eye for twenty years. On November 2, 1999 it showed up in New York. As it turns out, some experts examining the painting offered a new opinion on it. The painting may not have been painted by Rembrandt's hand but by that of one his students. The painting's subject may not be a rabbi. A new title for the piece is, *Portrait of a Man with Red Cape and Gold Chain.*

7.8 Golden Gate Park and The Black Doodler

Spreckels Lake, Golden Gate Park, 36th Avenue and Fulton, also John F. Kennedy Dr.
Crime: Serial Murder
Scene Status: The lake is still there

The Black Doodler is one of the more prolific serial killers who did not make a lot of headlines. The murderer is known to have been active in the city in the 1974-75 time frame. One victim attributed to the *Black Doodler* was Jae (Joe) Stephens. He was last seen in North Beach where he performed as a female impersonator. On June 25, 1974 Stephens was found stabbed to death in the bushes near Spreckels Lake in Golden Gate Park.

Privacy can be a powerful motivator. The news reports indicate at least one person could identify the suspect but did not come forward out of fear of compromising his status in the closet. The *Black Doodler* went to venues frequented by gay men, and offered to sketch the target. Once the two were alone he tried to kill them. He was successful and is attributed with 14 kills in the 1974-1975 two year period. One of San Francisco's most famous detectives, Rotea Gilford, worked on the case. As of 2020, no one has been brought to justice for the murders.

7.9 Golden Gate Park Body Dumps

Golden Gate Park
Crimes: Multiple Murders, Drugs, Prostitution
Scene Status: Minor changes to landscape

San Francisco's Golden Gate Park is an oasis in the middle of a major city. There are museums, botanical gardens, animals, exhibits, lakes and streams, playgrounds, and historical buildings. The oasis also has a lot of places to hide people and bodies.

In 1983 police found three people who were shot in the heads and sealed in steel drums dumped in San Francisco's Golden Gate Park. They were identified as Brenda Oakden, 19; Michael Thomas 24, and Phyllis Melendez, 20. They all had connections to drugs and prostitution. There is no official word on where in the park the bodies were found, but rumor places them near the buffalo paddocks.

Leaving fingerprints and palm prints on the barrel to dispose the victims is difficult to overcome. Police aimed their investigation at Anthony Sully. Sully was a former police officer for Millbrae (1966 to 1974), but working as an electrical contractor at the time. The murder victims had partied with the killer at his warehouse a few miles south. Drugs fit into the case as a motive and an enabler.

Sully was convicted in 1986 for killing three more women, bringing his total to five women and a man. One of his trials included him yelling in the court. The courts upheld his death sentence in 2013.

7.10 Golden Gate Park Polo Fields

Polo Fields, 1232 John F. Kennedy Dr. or Middle Dr. West
Crimes: Celebrity, Drugs, and Social Change
Scene Status: Fields still there

The Polo Fields in Golden Gate Park reflect moneyed tastes from when the park was built. There are few polo players left in the city, but during the 19th Century, a lot of wealthy San Franciscans were in the game. Now the polo fields served a lot of purposes including assembly sites. The track around the fields is 2/3 mile, and has been a velodrome since 1906.

On January 14, 1967 there was a massive concert at the Polo Fields. Before Manson and a whole lot of other people came to San Francisco and wore flowers in their hair, there was a lightning rod event called the, *Be In Concert*. The festival appealed to young disaffected youth; drugs, other disaffected youths, beautiful people, sex, and a warmth when much of the rest of the country was cold. Timothy Leary, and Allen Ginsberg were a few of the philosophical leaders of the *Be In*. Jefferson Airplane played. It was LSD's coming out party, and so many of the fans were tuning in and dropping out.

The *Summer of Love* followed in a few months because so many of those youth liked what they saw, and decided to come west to San Francisco; a place where people could put aside responsibility and address their priorities in life, like thinking and pleasure. The result was an influx of people, many of them without means, and more than a few predators.

7.11 The Beach Chalet

1000 Great Highway Great Highway, Golden gate Park at the Ocean
Crime: Drinking and Vice
Scene Status: The building has been remodeled and has new occupants

The Beach Chalet is a nice place to eat and drink with a beautiful view. It is at the Pacific Ocean end of Golden Gate Park. Now it houses a brewery, and a great restaurant. The structure was built in 1925 by the city of San Francisco, and was a recreation place. The downstairs had changing rooms for the beachgoers, and the upstairs had a restaurant to eat, and look out at the ocean. The building has a visitor's center on the ground floor, with a restaurant upstairs. The Works Progress Administration added beautiful murals and mosaics in the 1930's.

During Prohibition from 1920 to the end of 1933 alcohol was outlawed. Even with drink being illegal, there was no shortage of taverns available for a person to get a drink. The Beach Chalet was a great location for such a place because it was hidden at the end of Golden Gate Park. In 1932 a dozen men were arrested for lewdness when the occupying bar served alcohol and accompanied the booze with adult movies.

The facility was taken over by the US Army in WWII as part of the defenses for the city. In 1952 it hosted another party like 1932. Various tenants occupied the property and by the 1990's the city found a nice tenant to wipe away all of the past bad behavior and make it a pleasant venue to have a meal at a great location. The current iteration has a micro-brewery attached to it.

7.12 Sutro Baths

Point Lobos Ave. North end of Great Highway, Near the Cliff House and Palace of Fine Arts.

Crime: Arson

Scene Status: Concrete ruins remain, it is now a protected monument

The Sutro Bath Ruins feel like they should have hosted a lot of crimes, and over several epochs of time. The ruins are foundations built on a draw in the side of the cliffs looking out at the Pacific Ocean. While the stone foundations feel like ancient ruins, it only opened on March 14, 1896.

Adolph Sutro came a long way in life. He started in Germany and made his way to America. He was a genius and an innovator. The Nevada Silver Kings were his early clients when Sutro came up with a plan to drain the mines of their water. His idea made mining safer, and more profitable. Ralston was one of those clients.

Sutro became mayor of San Francisco from 1894 to 1896, but he continued to be a businessman. He set upon an idea to provide the people of San Francisco a recreation in the form of a massive swimming complex. It was near his Cliff House Restaurant. The entertainment complex became like an amusement park and could accommodate 10,000 visitors at a time. The venue had over 500 changing rooms. Admission was 25 cents, which included a rental bathing suit. The facility offered seven pools. There were warm pools, and cold pools, large and athletic pools. In later years the complex had curiosities on display like a stuffed animal zoo, and freak show. The facility was spectacular enough that Thomas Edison made a few short films of the baths after they opened in 1897.

Tastes changed and part of the complex was remade as an ice skating rink in 1937, with a full conversion in the 1950's. By the 1960's the facility was in decline, and not making a lot of money. A developer wanted to use the great location to build a condominium complex. The owners closed the facility in preparation for demolition. On June 26, 1966 a fire destroyed the complex. The buildings were a total loss. The cause was named arson. The developer collected the insurance money and left town. No one has been arrested for arson.

Right next door is the Cliff House, a restaurant with a great view out to the Pacific Ocean. It was also a project of Adolph Sutro. While it has burned down several times, and hosted numerous romantic trysts, it seems to be a non-crime scene. It is still a beautiful place.

7.13 The Hearth Bar

4701 Geary Blvd. and 11th Ave.
Crime: Alcohol, Fugitive, Murder, and Robbery
Scene Status: The Bar remains similar to as it was, with a large neon sign out front

The Hearth bar on Geary at 11th Ave. is a basic bar designed to be a comfortable neighborhood tavern for guests. It opened at 6:00 AM for the night-shifters going home.

In November of 1966 three well-dressed men came in, and drank for a while. Toward the end of the night, they got into a verbal altercation with a staffer and one of the men shot the staffer who died. The case was a robbery also, since the men stole money along with the homicide.

A trial resulted in convictions. One of the three suspects, William Asher, was sentenced to a work camp, where he escaped in 1975. Asher had 35 years of freedom which came to an end in 2011 when the FBI found him in Stanislaus County, a few hours east of San Francisco.

7.14 Hibernia Bank

Hibernia Bank, 1450 Noriega St., Northeast corner with 22nd St.
Crime: Celebrity, Kidnapping, Robbery, and Social Cause
Scene Status: New Bank occupies the remodeled location

Patty Hearst was San Francisco royalty. She grew up a part of the Hearst business empire. One of her family holdings included the San Francisco Examiner newspaper. San Francisco was home to many social movements, and when the Symbionese Liberation Army (SLA) came along it swept her up. On February 4, 1974 two men and a woman kidnapped her from her Berkeley apartment and indoctrinated her into the group by rape and torture. She was 19 years old. Ms. Hearst was indoctrinated in to the SLA by being tied up in a closet, and subjected to beatings and sexual assaults. After two months she seemed to be part of the group, and took the nom de guerre Tania.

On April 15, 1974, she was photographed wielding an M1 carbine while robbing the Hibernia Bank branch at 1450 Noriega Street. She worked with two men of the group. They stole $10,000 from the bank, and shot two bystanders in the process.

She later wrote a press release for the revolution providing her nom de guerre as Tania. The SLA Revolution demanded the Hearst family provide millions of dollars of food to needy Californians. The operation was called *People in Need*. The family complied by providing about $2,000,000, but the SLA deemed their efforts not good enough.

The FBI captured her in September of 1975 in a San Francisco apartment. F. Lee Bailey was her attorney and used the then new Stockholm Syndrome as a defense for Ms. Hearst. The court sentenced her to seven years in prison. She spent three years in prison before President Carter commuted her sentence and released her. President Clinton pardoned her in 2001.

7.15 Ocean View Motel

4340 Judah St. at La Playa St.
Crime: Celebrity, Death, and Drugs,
Scene Status: The overall motel scene is still there

Sublime front man Bradley Nowell met his end in a San Francisco motel room before the band became famous. *Sublime* was a Southern California band with a distinctive Reggae, surfer sound. They have also been classified at ska and punk. They started in 1988 and in the 1990's they became big and spawned other similar bands. Before they were big, they cut their signature album and embarked on a five-gig tour of the Bay Area.

News reports document when the band members woke on May 25th, 1996, they found Nowell dead. The autopsy revealed the cause of death was an opioid overdose. He was also reported to have had an opioid addiction. Bradley left behind a wife and child, as well as great music.

7.16 Ocean Beach

Beach, off the Great Highway, at Pacheco
Crime: Murder
Scene Status: The beach keeps changing over time

Ocean Beach, which is the strip on the ocean side of the San Francisco Peninsula, has a history of being the play land for the city. In the first half of the twentieth century, city dwellers came to the beach as a place of recreation. Along with the Sutro Baths and the Cliff House, people could go to the amusement park Playland and wander about Golden Gate Park.

Other things beside recreation happened at Ocean Beach. On December 24, 1973, detectives arrived to the beach near the area of the Great Highway and cross street Pacheco. There is a crosswalk there, for access from the nearby residential neighborhood. The scene was a grisly one, with a murder victim on the sand, wrapped in plastic and canvas. The body was headless, handless, and footless, as well as castrated. He became known as Unknown Body #169.

The police named him a victim of the Zebra Murders crime spree in 1973-4. (See 5.11) The detectives thought the victim was a homeless man taken from the Ghirardelli Square to be tortured, and dismembered prior to being dumped in the bay. He then washed up on the beach.

7.17 Zoo

San Francisco Zoo, Sloat Boulevard at Great Highway
Crime: Death by Animal Attack
Scene Status: Updated

The San Francisco Zoo is a great place to see animals near the beach. The zoo started in 1929 and was built largely by the boost of the Works Progress Administration during the 1930's. It was formerly called the Fleishhacker Zoo, after a benefactor. Homicide is a crime humans charge other humans with. The Zoo has been the site for two homicides where the killers were the animals.

On June 9, 1936, when the zoo was at its present location, and still called the Fleishhacker Zoo there was the first homicide. Wally the elephant attacked and killed his trainer. The animal was euthanized by court order.

Christmas Day 2007 was a busy day at the zoo. Three young men were visiting the zoo and spending time at the tiger cage. Tatiana was a 243 pound tiger enclosed in the cage, until she leapt over the 12 foot wall, and attacked three men. She attached the three and killed 17-year-old Carlos Sousa Jr. The other two men fled to the café around the corner, and the tiger tracked them there. The authorities confronted Tatiana, and put her down. There was a lot of finger pointing, and the citation of taunting, or nachos being part of the reason why the animal sought these men.

7.18 Lake Merced

1090 Lake Merced Blvd, Daly City
Crime: Celebrity, Death, and Dueling
Scene Status: A monument stands at the duel site

The Broderick and Terry duel came from two public figures' animosity toward each other. In the late 1850's dueling was outlawed in California but it did not stop two politicians from seeking satisfaction with their pistols.

David C. Broderick was born in Washington DC to Irish immigrant parents. He was an attorney and career politician who came to California after failing to get elected in New York. He assembled a political machine in San Francisco modeled after Tammany Hall in New York City. He had risen through California's state government to become the state's Senator in Washington. By the time of the duel, Broderick had been defeated in senatorial election.

David S. Terry was a lawyer from the south. He had become California's fourth Chief Justice, and helped write the state Constitution. He was pro-slavery. Terry's pro-slavery stance may have helped him lose an election, and at the time of event he was out of a job. Violence was not new to Terry; he had knifed a man only a few years before.

While the two opposed each other on the issue of slavery, politicians can often overlook matters to coexist. Both men were in the Democratic Party. But along the way, the opposition became personal and the two former friends and had a falling out. Terry perhaps felt the anti-slavery speeches of Broderick had damaged his electability. He gave a speech where he accused the delegates of following their master Broderick. Broderick felt betrayed and called

Terry an ingrate. Terry got wind of the name calling and demanded a retraction. Broderick told him to interpret the statements as he wished, and the two scheduled a duel.

Their first attempt at a duel was a failure since too many people showed up to watch and the police got wind of it and prevented the shootout. The two waited a few days and reschedule their duel near Lake Merced on September 13, 1859 near the San Francisco Zoo. The story goes Broderick was unfamiliar with the firearm, and pulled the trigger too early, shooting the ground. Terry landed a solid shot in Terry's torso. Broderick was taxied back to the Presidio where he died.

Broderick became a martyr for the antislavery cause. A street was named after him: there is no Terry Street. Famous detective Isiah Lees worked the case. He obtained a warrant to arrest Terry. When police arrived at Terry's house, he was holed up and said he would shoot it out if they came to get him. He agreed to surrender in three days. The authorities allowed him to do so, and he made good on his promise, appearing in Oakland court. The courts found Terry not guilty as he was in jeopardy at the time of the shooting. Terry met his end man years later when he tried to assault a judge, and the judge's security man shot him.

Bibliography

Adams, David F. *The Magnificent Rogues of San Francisco: A Gallery of Fakers and Frauds, Rascals and Robber Barons, Scoundrels and Scalawags.* Silver Stowe Books. 1998.

Arkin, Daniel and Corky Siemaszko. "Shooting of Kathryn Steinle: San Francisco pier killing suspect found not guilty of murder." *nbcnews.com.* December 1, 2017. Accessed May 19, 2020.

Asbury, Herbert. *The Barbary Coast: An Informal History of the San Francisco Underworld.* NY. Alfred A. Knopf. 1933.

Ball, Edward. *The Inventor and the Tycoon.* Doubleday. New York. 2013.

Bancroft, Hubert H. *History of California 1832. – 1918.* Archive.org. Accessed May 4, 2020.

Bay City News Service. "San Francisco: Man convicted of lighting sex partner's body on fire arrested for arson again" *Mercury News.* January 22, 2015. Accessed April 10. 2020.

Birmingham, Stephen. *California Rich: The Lives, the Times, the Scandals and the Fortunes of the Men and Women who made and Kept California's Wealth.* Simon and Schuster. New York. 1980.

Bishop, Katherine. "Haight-Ashbury Journal; Love and Hate Linger In Ex-Hippie District." *New York Times.* October 13, 1988.

Boessenecker, John. *Badge and Buckshot: Lawlessness in Old California.* University of Oklahoma Press. Norman OK. 1993.

Boulware, Jack. *San Francisco Bizzarro: A Guide to Notorious Sights, Lusty Pursuits, and Downright Freakiness in the City by the Bay.* St. Martin's Press. New York. 2000.

Bugliosi, Vincent. *Helter Skelter.* W. W. Norton and Co. 1974.

Callahan, Michael. "This Forgotten Day in San Francisco." April 8, 1965. *HoustonChronicle.com.* Hearst Media. April 7, 2015. Youtube.com video Accessed May 13, 2020.

Carpenter, Les. "The forgotten story of … Wyatt Earp and the 'fixed' heavyweight title fight." The Guardian. July 22, 2015. Accessed May 11, 2020.

Carroll, Jerry. "Tide Turns for the Beach Chalet / Storied ruin to get new life." *SFGate.com.* December 12, 1996. Accessed April 4, 2020.

Chamings, Andrew. The Death of an Actress. What Happened in Room 1219? *SFGate.com.* May 30, 2020. Accessed May 30, 2020.

BIBLIOGRAPHY

Chiang, Harriet. "10 YEARS AFTER / 101 California massacre victims helped toughen gun laws." *SFGate.com.* July 1, 2003. Accessed April 1, 2020.

Choy, Philip P. *San Francisco Chinatown: A Guide to its History and Architecture.* City Lights Bookstore. San Francisco. 2012.

Clarkson, Wesley. *Death at Every Stop.* St. Martin's. 1997.

CNNProfile. "Radically different: Heiress' life far removed from days of '74 kidnapping." *CNN.com.* June 28, 2012. Accessed May 12, 2020.

Correspondent, J. "Stolen Rembrandt is no Rembrandt and perhaps not a Rabbi." *JWeekly.com* August 25, 2000. Accessed May 1, 2020.

Crafts, Steven. "Barbary Coast." *FoundSF.org.* Accessed May 3, 2020.

Davis, Lisa. "A Killer Dies, a Mystery Lingers." *SFWeekly.com* September 6, 2000. Accessed April 29,2020.

Delgado, Ray. "Band's singer found dead in motel." *SFGate.com.* May 27, 1996. Accessed April 10, 2020.

Dickson, Samuel. *Tales of San Francisco.* Stanford University Press. Stanford, CA. 1947.

"Dispute over S.F. nightclub ends in Suicide." *SFGATE.com.* August 12, 1996. Accessed April 17, 2020.

Dorfman, Zachary. "The Secret History of the Russian Consulate in San Francisco." *Foreignpolicy.com.* December 14, 2017.

Doyle, J D. https://www.queermusicheritage.com/drag-bourbon.html Article on Rae Bourbon. Accessed April 1, 2020.

Drexler, Paul. "I Left My Crime Family in San Francisco." *SFExaminer.com.* December 20, 2015. Accessed May 9, 2020.

Drexler, Paul. "Joseph Duncan, Bank Wrecker." *SFExaminer.com.* April 9, 2017. Accessed May 12, 2020.

Duke, Thomas S. *Celebrated Criminal Cases of America.* James H. Barry Co. San Francisco CA. 1910.

"Dynamite Outrages: Two Men Arrested in San Francisco by Police. *New York Times.* February 17, 1887. Accessed May 20, 2020 at cable-car-guy.com.

Eskenazi, Joe. "Terry Helbling's Tenderloin Flat Full of $200K in Stolen Art." *SFWeekly.com.* March 9, 2011. Accessed May 5, 2020.

Fagan, Kevin and Jaxon Van Derbeken. "3 kids feared dead -- thrown into S.F. bay / Mother who said she heard voices is arrested -- child's body is recovered near Fort Mason." *SFGate.com.* October 20, 2005. Accessed May 22, 2020.

Fernandez, Lisa. "News Crew Mugged, Cameras Stolen at San Francisco Pier." *Nbcbayarea.com.* July 2, 2015. Accessed April 9, 2020.

Ferrero, Bill. "Mysterious fire ended Sutro Baths and condo plan." *SFGate.com.* October 11, 1999. Accessed May 3, 2020.

Fimrite, Peter. "Lamborghini Thief Max Wade Given Life for Botched Killing." *SFGate.com.* January 23, 2014. Accessed April 18, 2020.

Finkel, Michael. *True Story: Murder, Memoir, Mea Culpa.* HarperCollins. NY. 2005.

Graysmith, Robert. *The Sleeping Lady: The Trailside Murders Above the Golden Gate.* Dutton Books. New York. 1990.

Greenberg, Andy. "In Silk Road Appeal, Ross Ulbricht's Defense Focuses on Corrupt Feds." *Wired.* January 12, 2016. Accessed April 18, 2020.

Hanisee, Michele. "Death Penalty Exhausted Appeals – Part 6." *Citizen's Journal.* https://www.citizensjournal.us. May 20, 2019. Accessed May 10, 2020.

Harrell, Ashley. "Lance Farber, Arsonist Beau of S.F. Planning Chief John Rahaim, Dies at 49." *SFWeekly.com.* April 20, 2010. Accessed April 25, 2020.

Hatfield, Larry D. "Bar owner sought in shooting." *SFGATE.com.* July 26, 1996. Accessed April 8, 2020.

History.com Editors. "Patty Hearst captured." *A&E Television Networks.* February 9, 2010. Accessed April 13, 2020.

Hoeper, George. *Black Bart, Boulevardier Bandit: The Saga of California's Most Mysterious Stagecoach Robber and the Men Who Sought to Capture Him.* Word Dancer Press. Fresno CA. 1995.

Jamison, Peter. "Weathermen's Ticking Time Bomb." *LA Weekly.* September 15, 2009. Accessed April 10, 2020.

Japan Weekly Mail. Yokohama. Vol 1, #42. November 10, 1877. Accessed March 25, 2020.

Kamiya, Gary. "S.F. 'Boss' Abe Ruef took unusual route to power." *SFChronicle.com.* July 3, 2015. Accessed May 1, 2020.

Lee, Henry K. *Taxi Driver Sent to Mental Hospital for Murder. SFGate.com.* August 4, 2009. Accessed April 24, 2020.

Lefebvre, Sam. "Without Charles Sullivan, There'd Be No Fillmore As We Know It." *KQED.org.* June 14, 2017. Accessed April 10, 2020.

Lindsey, Robert. "Dan White, Killer of San Francisco Mayor, A Suicide." *New York Times.* Oct. 22, 1985. Accessed May 5, 2020.

Lovinger, Paul W. "Original Hindu Temple in USA is overhauled after 111 years." *MarinaTimes.com.* March 2017. Accessed April 10, 2020.

"Man found guilty of involuntary manslaughter in Buena Vista Park choking death" *SFExaminer.com.* Aug. 27, 2014. Accessed April 11, 2020.

BIBLIOGRAPHY

Mintz, Howard. "Former Peninsula cop's death sentence upheld in bodies-in-barrels murder case." *Mercury News.* August 6, 2013. Accessed April 10, 2020.

Mojadad, Ida. "'Doodler' Back in Limelight Despite No Updates to Case: Police still haven't connected the five 1970s murders of gay men in the Castro to the 'Doodler' but everyone else has." *SFWeekly.* June 21, 2018. Accessed March 11, 2020.

Newton, Michael. *The Second Edition of The Encyclopedia of Serial Killers.* "Wyatt Earp." Checkmark Books. 2006.

Rego, Nilda "Days Gone By: Wyatt Earp, boxing referee, makes a controversial call." *Contra Costa Times. January 24, 2010.* Accessed May 2, 2020.

NPS.gov "Golden Gate National Recreation Area." Accessed May 3, 2020.

O'Brien, Robert. *This is San Francisco: A Classic Portrait of the City.* Chronicle Books. San Francisco. 1994.

Orr, James. "Victims 'taunted tiger' before it killed zoo visitor." *TheGuardian.com.* January 18, 2008. Accessed May 15, 2020.

Orth, Maureen. *Vulgar Favors: Andrew Cunanan, Gianni Versace, and the Largest Failed Manhunt in US History.* Delacorte Press. New York. 1999.

Paddock, Richard C. "Moscow Says Flashy Diamond Merchant Stole $180 Million. *Los Angeles Times.* June 20, 1998. Accessed April 16, 2020.

PBS. "Alcatraz Is Not an Island: The Occupation 1969-1971." http://www.pbs.org/itvs/alcatrazisnotanisland/occupation.html. Preserved on WaybackMachine.com dated December 22, 2002. Accessed April 24, 2020.

Pereira, Alyssa. "The Scandalous History Behind the Great American Music Hall." *7x7.com.* March 25, 2014. Accessed May 3, 2020.

Perry, George. *San Francisco In the Sixties.* Pavilion Books. London. 2001.

Peterson, Art. "The Sentinel Building." *FoundSF.org.* Accessed April 30, 2020.

Polk, Jim. "Jones plotted cyanide deaths years before Jonestown,".*CNN.com.* November 12, 2008. Accessed May 10, 2020.

Read, Simon. *War of Words: A True Tale of Newsprint and Murder.* Sterling Publishing Co. New York. 2009.

Rehlaender, Jamie L. *A Howl of Free Expression: the 1957 Howl Obscenity Trial and Sexual Liberation.* Portland State University. Young Historians' Conference 2015.

"'Religious Reasons' Cited – Murder Suspects Admit Slayings," The Press-Courier (Oxnard, Ca.), Apr. 28, 1983. Accessed on http://unknownmisandry.blogspot.com May 20, 2020.

Reynolds, Richard. *Cry For War, The Story of Suzan and Michael Carson.* Create Space Press. 1988.

Richards, Leonard L. *The California Gold Rush and the Coming of the Civil War*. Alfred A. Knopf. New York. 2007.

Richards, Rand. *Historic Walks in San Francisco: 18 Trails Through the City's Past*. Heritage House. San Francisco. 2008.

Rossen, Jake. "The Man Who Built a 40-Foot Spite Fence Around His Neighbor's Home." *Mentalfloss.com*. April 24, 2017. Accessed May 4, 2020.

Rubenstein, Steve. "Escaped Tiger Kills Visitor to S. F. Zoo." *San Francisco Chronicle*. December 26, 2007. Accessed April 22, 2020.

Sanfrancsicotheatres.blogspot.com/2017. "SF Theatres: Hippodrome 560 Pacific"

Sanders, Prentice Earl and Ben Cohen. *The Zebra Murders: A Season of Killing, Racial Madness and Civil Rights*. Simon & Schuster. 2006.

Schulten, Susan. "San Francisco Mapped Every Brothel, Opium Den, and Gambling Parlor During a Moral Panic in the 1880s: The ugly motive behind a beautiful diagram of old Chinatown ." *NewRepublic.com*. July 2, 2014. Accessed April 25, 2020.

Secrest, William. *Dark and Tangled Threads of Crime. San Francisco's Famous Police Detective, Isaiah W. Lees*. Word Dancer Press. Sanger CA. 2004.

Sherman, William Tecumseh. *Personal Memoirs of General W. T. Sherman*. D. Appleton And Company. New York. 1889. Second Ed. Accessed at Gutenberg.org. May 4, 2020.

"Shoot Elephant Despite Protest" "Huge Beast That Killed Keeper Put to Death By Police With Moose Guns" *News and Observer*. Raleigh NC. June 19, 1936.

Silverman, Victor and Susan Stryker. *Screaming Queens*. *http://www.screamingqueensmovie.com*. Accessed April 20, 2020.

Simerman, John. "Porn King Jim Mitchell Dead at 63." *Mercury News*. July 15, 2007. Accessed May 20, 2020.

Smith, Ian. Filmed by Edison in 1897, this footage shows San Francisco's iconic "Sutro Baths" *TheVintageNews.com*. June 15, 2016. Accessed May 14, 2020.

Staff. Ferguson, William I. *http://www.joincalifornia.com/candidate/10615*. Accessed April 17, 2020.

Staff. "Sutro Baths History". *https://www.nps.gov/goga/learn/historyculture/sutro-baths.htm*. National Park Service. Accessed April 5, 2020.

Staff Reports. "1985: Angry mob captures Night Stalker suspect Richard Ramirez." *El Paso Times*. September 1, 1985. Accessed May 5, 2020.

Stanford, Sally with Bob Patterson. *The Lady of the House*. G. P. Putnam's Sons, New York. 1966.

Talbot, David. *The Season of the Witch*. Simon and Schuster. 2012.

BIBLIOGRAPHY

Tefertiller, Casey. *Wyatt Earp: The Life behind the Legend.* John Wiley and Sons. New York. 1997.

Turner, Alford E. Editor. *The Earps Talk.* Creative Publishing Company. College Station TX. 1980.

Van Derbeken, Jaxon. "Why jury called it murder / Negligence, deception cited in mauling trial." *SFGate.com.* March 22, 2002. Accessed March 1, 2020.

Vega, Cecilia M. "Landmark fire chief's residence is vandalized." *SFGate.com.* February 24, 2008. Accessed April 23, 2020.

VerdantPress.com. "Six Gallery." Accessed May 10, 2020.

Walsh, Ed. "Man convicted in SF's infamous dog mauling case dies." *Bay Area Reporter.* November 14, 2018. Accessed May 20, 2020.

Westcott, Kathryn. "What is Stockholm syndrome?" *BBC News Magazine.* August 22, 2013. Accessed May 4, 2020.

Wright, Benjamin Cooper. *Banking in California 1849-1910.* San Francisco: H. S. Crocker Co. 1910.

Ziv, Stav. "Chronicle Founder shot dead in feud, 1880. *SFGate.com.*" December 9, 2012. Accessed December 5, 2015.

Index

INDEX

INDEX

INDEX

INDEX

Author Bio

Eric Golembiewski is the author of *Crime Scene Decisions*, *The Decisive Investigator*, *Someone's Always Cooking in Penang*, and other books. He studied Military History at LSU, worked as a detective, and lived in San Francisco for a time.

www.ingramcontent.com/pod-product-compliance
Lightning Source LLC
Chambersburg PA
CBHW050729030426
42336CB00012B/1480